GUTS & GLORY

THE AMERICAN REVOLUTION

GUTS & GLORY

THE AMERICAN REVOLUTION

BEN THOMPSON

ILLUSTRATIONS BY
C. M. BUTZER

Little, Brown and Company

New York   Boston

Little, Brown and Company
Hachette Book Group
1290 Avenue of the Americas, New York, NY 10104
Visit us at lb-kids.com

First Edition: June 2017

Little, Brown and Company is a division of Hachette Book Group, Inc. The Little, Brown name and logo
are trademarks of Hachette Book Group, Inc.

The publisher is not responsible for websites (or their content) that are not owned by the publisher.

Library of Congress Cataloging-in-Publication Data
Names: Thompson, Ben, 1980– author | Butzer, C. M., illustrator.
Title: The American Revolution / Ben Thompson ; Illustrations by C. M. Butzer.
Description: New York : Little, Brown and Company, 2017. | Series: Guts & glory ; vol. 1 | Includes
bibliographical references and index.
Identifiers: LCCN 2016030632| ISBN 9780316312097 (hardcover) | ISBN 9780316312103 (ebook) |
ISBN 9780316312080 (library edition ebook)
Subjects: LCSH: United States—History—Revolution, 1775-1783—Juvenile literature.
Classification: LCC E208 .T465 2017 | DDC 973.3—dc23
LC record available at https://lccn.loc.gov/2016030632

ISBNs: 978-0-316-31209-7 (hardcover), 978-0-316-31210-3 (ebook)

Printed in the United States of America

LSC-C

10 9 8 7 6

The tree of liberty must be refreshed from time to time with the blood of patriots and tyrants.

—**Thomas Jefferson**

CONTENTS

Gentlemen may cry, Peace, peace! But there is no peace. The war is actually begun! The next gale that sweeps from the north will bring to our ears the clash of resounding arms! Our brethren are already in the field! Why stand we here idle? What is it that gentlemen wish? What would they have? Is life so dear, or peace so sweet, as to be purchased at the price of chains and slavery? Forbid it, Almighty God! I know not what course others may take; but as for me, give me liberty or give me death!

—Patrick Henry, speech to the Second Virginia Convention, 1775

Being taxed to death by a king who lives three thousand miles away doesn't sit too well with Boston agitator Samuel Adams. So he and his buddies decide that a little civil disobedience will show the king what he's dealing with.

Introduction

Origins of a Rebellion

Three millions of people, armed in the holy cause of Liberty, and in such a country as that which we possess, are invincible by any force which our enemy can send against us.

—Patrick Henry, March 23, 1775

WHAT IF I TOLD YOU THAT THE STORY about George Washington cutting down a cherry tree is total crap, and that once, GW swore at a dude so much that the entire Continental Army stopped running away and turned to face a British bayonet charge? And what if I told you that Thomas Jefferson, the third president of the United States (and the guy on the nickel), had a panic attack when he found out he was supposed to write the Declaration of Independence? Seriously, Ben Franklin and John Adams had to chase him into a bar and drink beers with him until he finally decided, "Okay, yeah, I will write a letter to the dang king of England telling him to suck lemons."

Did you know that Andrew Jackson, the man on the twenty-dollar bill, joined the army at the age of thirteen, was captured by the British, and was so disrespectful to the officer who captured him that the dude chopped part of Jackson's hand off with a sword? Oh yeah, and what if I told you the greatest war hero of the American Revolution ended up turning traitor and joining the British? Now we have three monuments in his honor in the United States, but he's so hated that none of them actually mention his name.

The American Revolution is, without question, the single most important event in American history. It was the longest war the US has ever fought, it killed 1 percent of the American population (which might not sound like much, but it's a really big number of people), and it altered the course of human history forever. Victory in the American Revolution set up the first democracy in the modern world—you know, the system of government where people actually get to vote for things—and it marked the end of the old days, when the king or the queen basically forced the royal subjects to do whatever he or she wanted.

Now, there were a lot of things going on that led to war between America and Great Britain, but the short version is that the Americans didn't want to pay taxes to the British king. So they pulled out a bunch of guns and started threatening government officials. The British didn't back down, because they felt like the American colonies *should* pay taxes, and then all heck broke loose.

But we're getting a little ahead of ourselves here. Let's back up 160 years or so to when the English first came to America. As much as the director of your school Thanksgiving play loves to talk about Pilgrims and Plymouth Rock and eating giant turkeys stuffed with cranberry sauce and bacon, the first English settlement in the New World was actually at Jamestown, Virginia, in 1607. Thirteen years later, the Pilgrims landed at Plymouth Rock and started baking candied yams, and then over the next hundred years or so, more and more English settlements started popping up all over the place, from Rhode Island to Georgia.

Eventually, America was divided into thirteen colonies, each with its own governor: Connecticut, Delaware, New Hampshire, Massachusetts, New York, New Jersey, Pennsylvania, Rhode Island, Virginia, Maryland, North Carolina, South Carolina, and Georgia. Present-day Vermont was part of New Hampshire, and Maine was part of Massachusetts. People living in the colonies were considered British subjects, under the rule of the king of England and the protection of the British Army, and laws were made by the king and the British Parliament, which is like their version of our present-day Congress.

America was a good place for people from England to go to live because England was super-crowded and really expensive. Over in America there was a ton of cheap land people could buy for farming or ranching or whatever. When your options are "work in a horrible factory or at a smelly dock for very little money in England" or "own a couple of acres of land and sit on your back porch in the middle of nowhere in America," many people chose to travel across the Atlantic Ocean to try to build a new life. The only thing you really had to worry about in North America was that occasionally a bunch of American Indians would come to try to kill you because you were technically stealing *their* land. But most Colonial villages set up groups called militias, which were neighborhood armies, kind of like a cross between a volunteer fire department and a US Army National Guard infantry battalion.

England wasn't the only European country that had colonists living in America. The British colonies were basically just the East Coast of the modern-day United States. Florida, Texas, Mexico, and most of South America were held by Spain, and the French colonists lived in Quebec, Canada, and on a humongous chunk of land just west of the Appalachian Mountains (this territory was called Louisiana, but it actually stretched from New Orleans all the way up to Detroit and was way bigger than the current state of Louisiana).

As you might imagine, England, France, and Spain all

occupying North America at the same time eventually caused problems, and before long there was a huge war.

The fight actually started in Europe and had literally nothing to do with America. In 1756, Queen Maria Theresa of Austria went to war with the German state of Prussia over a little chunk of land called Silesia. Austria and Prussia called their buddies to help them, and before long you had an epic war, with Austria, Russia, Spain, Sweden, and France on one side and Prussia, Great Britain, and Portugal on the other. A lot of those countries had colonies that bordered each other in other parts of the world, too, so then you had guys fighting in India, the Caribbean, North America, and anywhere else.

In Europe, people refer to this humongous world war as the Seven Years' War, but in America we call our part in it the French and Indian War, because it actually only lasted four years, and over here the British colonists were fighting against the French and the American Indians. This makes it easier to keep track of.

The details of the French and Indian War could make a whole other book, but here's the deal: The British Army came to America and kicked France's booty, beating them up and down the Mississippi and in Canada. Then, over in Europe, the British Royal Navy smoked the French Navy into burning cinders, blasting apart their ships, crippling their sea power for decades, and making it really hard for them to bring fresh troops across the ocean. The American colonists contributed their small groups of militia soldiers to the British cause, but the colonists had very little formal military training (and zero experience fighting as regular infantry), so for the most part these farmer-soldiers ran away every time they had to fight actual French Army forces. This cheesed off the British a little, and eventually they stopped using Colonial militias to help them fight in important battles.

The French and Indian War ended with the Treaty of Paris in 1763, which basically kicked the French out of North America once and for all. All French holdings in Canada went to England. All French holdings along the Mississippi went to Spain. Florida became a British colony, and England also took territory in India and the Caribbean from the French. It was a crushing victory.

Well, for all the glory and heroism and butt-kicking, England ended the war with a little bit of a problem. Wars are really expensive and require a ton of money to pay soldiers and keep them fighting. So the British figured since they'd basically just fought a big war in America to protect the American colonists from the French and the American Indians, the American colonists should cough up some taxes to help, you know, actually pay for it.

On the surface this might make sense, but there's a problem: America didn't have any seats in the British Parliament, so the colonists felt like they were stuck doing whatever

**Eastern North America in 1775. The British controlled
the middle and right portions of the map, and Spain
controlled the left portion.**

England decided they should do. The Americans didn't have
a single vote in the matter, and now they were going to be
forced to pay all this money to the king over a war they didn't
start—and that took place mostly on another continent. This
made some folks in the colonies a little super-righteously
furiously angry. (We'll see how that plays out in chapter 1.)

When war finally broke out between the American colonists and Great Britain, each side had very distinct advantages and disadvantages:

GREAT BRITAIN

In 1775, Great Britain was the single most powerful country in the world. The British Empire was made up of England, Scotland, Ireland, Canada, the Bahamas, Jamaica, Grenada, and Barbados, as well as parts of Africa and India and even China, and it stretched across every continent on Earth (even Antarctica!). It consisted of millions of people and had a nearly limitless supply of money coming in. It had the largest, best-trained, and most powerful navy in the world, and an army that had proved itself time after time on the battlefield. The British hadn't lost a war in over a hundred years, and they'd hardly lost a single battle in the Seven Years' War.

Of course, for a war in America, they would need to transport everything three thousand miles across the Atlantic Ocean, and they would need to keep resources available to defend their holdings in Africa, India, the Caribbean, and even back home in England. There were a lot of angry countries— particularly France and Spain—that were just looking for an opportunity to shank the English in the back while they were focusing on a war with the American colonists.

THE AMERICAN COLONIES

In the early years of the Revolution, America had no formal government, no army, no navy, and very few actual cities. Despite being a gigantic chunk of land, America actually had, like, half as many people living in it as there were in England, meaning that America had far fewer soldiers to throw into combat. The Americans also had no formal currency, no way to pay for things, and few experienced military commanders. They'd fought poorly in the French and Indian War, and no American force had proved it could stand toe-to-toe with a European army on the battlefield.

Even worse, the country was divided among three distinct groups of people: the patriots (guys who were actively fighting in the rebellion), the loyalists (people who were actively fighting on the side of the British because they didn't want to break away from the British Empire), and people who refused to fight for either side. Still, despite this division and all these drawbacks, the Americans had a few advantages: They were fighting on their home turf, they knew the roads and the land, and they believed in the cause. And home field advantage can make all the difference.

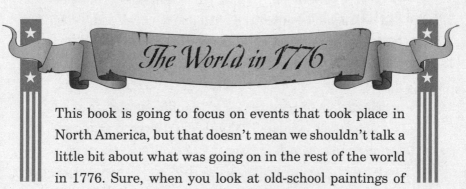

The World in 1776

This book is going to focus on events that took place in North America, but that doesn't mean we shouldn't talk a little bit about what was going on in the rest of the world in 1776. Sure, when you look at old-school paintings of people from the 1700s, they all look pretty chill. But in reality the world was a messed-up place filled with secret political dealings, powerful personalities, and tons of crazy drama.

Western Europe was the dominant power in the world at this time, and every country on the European Continent was working hard to build huge military and trade empires stretching across the globe (think of it like an epic, real-life version of *Civ*). They were constantly switching alliances and backstabbing each other for their own gain. It was a brutal, double-crossing world full of wars, assassinations, spies, and deceit.

Ruled by the might of King George III, England was the primary power in Europe, having just come out on top of the Seven Years' War. Scotland was technically its own country, connected to England by something called the Acts of Union. While they still had to do what the English king and Parliament told them, the Scots also had a bunch of seats in the Parliament, so it wasn't like they didn't get a vote. (This setup is kind of what the Americans were hoping for when they first started the Revolution.) Ireland was also connected to England, although a lot of Irish people were unhappy about this.

Altogether, Scotland, Wales, and England made up Great Britain, which was the union of all three countries under the power of King George III. Yes, it's just as confusing as it sounds, and to make it worse, I'm mostly going to use *England* and *Great Britain* to mean pretty much the same thing throughout this book. Plus, don't forget that the British Empire included huge chunks of land in North America (the American colonies), the Caribbean, Africa, and India, meaning the king of England had a lot of power and control in those countries, too.

In England, Edward Gibbon had just published the first volume of his massive epic, *The History of the Decline and Fall of the Roman Empire*. Intrepid explorer James Cook was setting out on his final voyage, the one where he became the first European to set foot on the Hawaiian Islands (and shortly thereafter became the first European to be killed by a Hawaiian warrior). Scottish economist Adam Smith had published the rule book for capitalism, *The Wealth of Nations*, and inventor James Watt had just refined the steam engine—an invention that changed the world forever and helped kick-start a period known as the Industrial Revolution. Another noteworthy invention arrived around this time as well, when Scotsman Alexander Cummings invented a key component of what would eventually become the modern flush toilet. Sure, you laugh, but think about where we'd be without *that* one.

France was in the second year of the reign of King Louis XVI and his wife, Queen Marie Antoinette. They were the last king and queen of France and were overthrown and publicly beheaded by their subjects a few years after the American Revolution. France had been considered the largest and most powerful army in Europe but had recently been humbled by the butt-kicking it received in the Seven Years' War. France was now desperately trying to rebuild the shattered remnants of its army and navy. It still held Haiti (known as Saint-Domingue at the time), Saint Lucia, Martinique, and Guadeloupe in the Caribbean but had lost most of its holdings in India and all of its lands in America. France desperately wanted to avenge its honor against England but didn't have the means to do so.

Within the country, writers of the French Enlightenment such as Voltaire and Diderot were publishing works saying that individual freedom, equality, science, and reason should replace the old way of kings and the Catholic Church, which dominated every aspect of people's lives. These authors' works were read extensively by the American Founding Fathers, who tried to apply them to the Revolution.

Spain was ruled by King Carlos III, who was a cousin of French king Louis XVI. Carlos was an enlightened, intelligent leader who tried to improve his country, encouraging the works of influential artists such as Francisco Goya. But it was clear that the once-mighty empire of Spain was now in decline. It still held Cuba, the Dominican Republic, Puerto Rico, the Philippines, Mexico, Texas, Louisiana, and huge parts of South America, but Spanish subjects in those regions were getting cranky. Spain was also expanding into the California Territory, having just established the towns of San Francisco and Tucson in 1776. There was a lot of unrest in these territories, though, primarily from the native peoples in Mexico and South America. The idea of rebellious North American colonies overthrowing the English king was terrifying to the Spanish Crown.

Other European powers were working on their own colonies as well. Portugal had colonized Brazil and many territories on the west coast of Africa, and the expert trading and merchant kingdom of the Netherlands held Saint Eustatius in the Caribbean, as well as Cape Colony (South Africa) and the Dutch East Indies (Indonesia and parts of what is now Malaysia).

Neither Germany nor Italy existed as a country at the time—they were both just big messes of little countries and states that sort of spoke the same language. The most powerful German state was Prussia, which had won amazing victories under its king, Frederick the Great, in the Seven Years' War. Afterward, many of these German states, particularly Hesse-Kassel, offered to lend their highly experienced armies to the highest bidder. These hired soldiers were called mercenaries, and England bought tens of thousands of Hesse-Kassel soldiers to help in the war against America, which made the Americans *very* mad.

Austria was in the twenty-sixth year of the reign of Queen Maria Theresa, queen of Austria, Hungary, and Croatia. Maria was the mother of the French queen, Marie Antoinette, and the two countries were in an alliance at the moment. Many people in Maria Theresa's kingdom were reading the works of best-selling German writer Johann Wolfgang von Goethe, and they were flocking to packed concert halls to hear the music of Josef Haydn and an up-and-coming twenty-year-old composer named Wolfgang Amadeus Mozart.

Poland was in trouble in 1776. Four years earlier it had been pressured into the First Partition of Poland, where basically the entire country was divided up among Prussia, Austria, and Russia. The Polish tried to resist, primarily under the leadership of a heroic nobleman named Casimir Pulaski, but the rebellion was crushed. The once-proud Polish-Lithuanian Commonwealth was at the mercy of its neighbors.

Russia, meanwhile, was doing the best it had done in decades. The powerful Empress Catherine the Great was in charge, with her armies commanded by military genius Alexander Suvorov. Russia had won huge victories against Poland and the Ottoman Turkish Empire in recent years. It was also modernizing its army, building a navy, and trying to get rid of slavery, and had recently taken huge chunks of Ukraine and the Crimea from Turkish control.

The Ottoman Turks under Sultan Abdul Hamid I controlled Iraq, Syria, Egypt, and pretty much all of the Middle East, but this was another empire in slow decline. The Turks' defeat by the Russians in 1774 was humiliating, and rebellions in various Middle Eastern provinces were causing more and more trouble for the sultan, who was barely maintaining control of his empire.

Farther south, Iran (which was called Persia until 1935) was controlled by the Zand Dynasty. Twenty years before, Persia had been run by the great conqueror Nader Shah, a brutal military dictator who idolized Genghis Khan and exterminated rivals across the Middle East and India. But with Nader Shah's death in 1747, his empire pretty much fell apart immediately. It was taken over by one of his top generals, Karim Khan, but after his death the empire devolved into fighting and bickering and broke apart completely.

India was being hit hard by the Europeans in 1776, particularly the forces of the British East India Company. England had forcibly taken control of many port cities in India and was now making tons and tons of cash by sending exotic spices and other items back to Europe. France and Holland had tried to break into the market, but England fought them off and kept its vise grip on the world's most expensive resources. The rest of the Indian subcontinent was technically divided between the crumbling Muslim Mughal Empire and the Hindu Maratha

Empire, but neither lasted long against the might of the British Empire.

China had over 13 million square miles of territory and over 300 million people and was ruled by the Qianlong Emperor of the Qing Dynasty. In 1776, China was one of the largest, richest, and most culturally advanced civilizations in the world. The emperor was promoting literature and culture and was building epic Buddhist temples and the largest library in the world. But he also ruthlessly exterminated his enemies in Mongolia, Tibet, and Burma in a series of military conquests known as the "Ten Great Campaigns."

Japan was in the 173rd year of the Tokugawa Shogunate government. Under the rule of Emperor Go-Momozono and Shogun Tokugawa Ieharu, Japan was in the era of "Peaceful Eternity," part of a long-running golden age of tranquility that had begun back in 1615. But Japan had sealed its borders against all foreigners and did not permit trade or outside visitors at all.

Author's Note

It is not in the still calm of life, or in the repose of a
pacific station, that great characters are formed.

—Abigail Adams, wife of John Adams and First Lady
of the United States

MY FIFTH GREAT-GRANDFATHER, THOMAS
Jennings (1746–1812), came to the Colony of
Virginia as an indentured servant at the age of thir-
teen. By 1776, he was thirty years old, five years younger than
I am now, and he already owned his own farm in Spotsylvania
County. He had just married a woman named Sarah Carter,
but when the call came for soldiers to fight for American free-
dom, Jennings left his family and his home, enlisted in the
army, and served throughout the war as a rifleman in Captain
John Herndon's company of the Virginia Militia. I don't have

a list of engagements he served in, but in addition to fighting as a soldier, he also—according to the documentation I have—"supplied beef." I have no idea what that means, but I like to envision him having totally jacked arms and punching people while saying "Here comes the *beef*!"

Even though this war was fought 241 years ago, the American Revolution seems to follow me around pretty much everywhere I go. I was born in downtown Philadelphia, two blocks from the Liberty Bell. I was named after my great-grandfather, who was named after Benjamin Franklin. My dad used to have a Brown Bess and a Pennsylvania rifle hanging on the wall of our living room, right next to a portrait of George Washington, and my pops used to impress his friends at parties because I could identify all three things by name when I was still a baby. He also did his senior history thesis at the University of Virginia on British Lieutenant Colonel Banastre Tarleton (a guy I'll talk about in detail in chapter 19). Tarleton almost succeeded in kidnapping Thomas Jefferson, who founded the University of Virginia, so I don't know what this says about Dad's school spirit.

I can do the Patrick Henry "give me liberty or give me death" speech from memory because my mom would recite it every time my brother and I were driving her completely crazy. At my first "grown-up" job, working as a file clerk in some tiny Massachusetts law firm, I could look out the window of my cubicle and see the spot where the Boston Massacre went down. I once played in a softball game in the park across the street from the Bunker Hill monument. I've walked the streets of Colonial Williamsburg, accidentally discovered the battlefield at Cowpens while searching for a gas station, visited the Declaration of Independence in Washington, DC, and walked the parapets of Fort Independence in Massachusetts Bay.

Heck, I've reenacted battles from the Revolutionary War, fired a flintlock musket, and felt the weight of a loaded powder box on my shoulder. I have an exact replica of Lord Cornwallis's red army coat hanging in my closet right now, and every time I'm too lazy to think of a good Halloween costume, I slap that together with a powdered wig, some dark makeup, and a tricorne hat and go as Zombie Cornwallis. As you might imagine, this costume sometimes requires a little explaining.

What I'm saying is that for me this stuff isn't just ancient history buried in the pages of a dusty textbook so boring it can be used as a form of torture. The American Revolution is part of every single aspect of our lives, whether you're voting for a class president, saying the Pledge of Allegiance, signing a petition, or handing a cashier a ten-dollar bill. You can still see leftovers of the Revolution in street names, monuments, money, and statues all across the United States, and in TV shows like *TURN* and video games like *Assassin's Creed III* and *Fallout 4*. And, as much as 1776 feels like an eternity ago, think about this for a minute: America has been a country for just over 240 years. When we became a nation, Great Britain had existed for more than seven hundred years. Before that, the Romans were around for over a thousand years, and the Chinese emperors reigned for more than *two thousand*. America is a blip on the timeline of world history, and the Revolution was not as long ago as you might think.

With this book I wanted to tell the story of the American Revolution from beginning to end, highlighting white-knuckled acts of incredible bravery, from epic battles, to sword-swinging mayhem, to fearless spy missions, to high-octane bayonet charges. But I also wanted to highlight the heroism of progressive thinkers like Thomas Jefferson, John Adams, and many others who were trying to figure out a brand-new system of government that had never been successfully tried before. There are some stories you'll know and others that I bet will surprise you. Either way, it's going to be a heck of a journey from the riotous streets of Boston, to the bloodstained shores of Yorktown, to the very beginning of the country that we are lucky to live in today.

All right, let's do this.

The Sons of Liberty

The "Iron Man of the People" Throws the Redcoats a Tea Party They Won't Soon Forget

Boston, Massachusetts
1765–1774

> Among the natural rights of the Colonists are these:
> First, a right to life; Secondly, to liberty; Thirdly,
> to property; together with the right to support and
> defend them in the best manner they can.
>
> —Samuel Adams, American patriot

THE AMERICAN REVOLUTION BEGAN IN the same place where many of the all-time greatest *Dungeons and Dragons* campaigns have started: a cool, old-school, wood-paneled tavern, lit by candles and full of all kinds of seedy outlaws.

It's fitting, then, that one of the great rabble-rousers of American independence was a dude who is now best known for having a brand of beer named after him.

Samuel Adams was born September 27, 1722, in the big-time port city of Boston, Massachusetts. After finishing grade school at the age of fourteen (you only had to go to school until you were fourteen in those days, which sounds pretty nice to me), Sam got accepted to Harvard. There he wrote his thesis paper about why it should be totally okay if the colonies didn't want to listen to every dumb thing King George III of England said. And even though this wasn't a mega-popular topic for Sammy to be writing about in 1743, he didn't care. If there's one thing you will learn about Sam Adams in this book, it's that this guy was white-hot intense about pretty much everything. Once he got his mind set on something, there was really nothing that you or the king or an army or anybody else could do to stop him.

As far as Adams was concerned, decisions about America should be made by Americans, not a Parliament and a king who lived on the other side of the planet.

It's worth looking at this whole situation from the point of view of the British for a second, though. Remember what I said in the introduction about the French and Indian War? Well, in the years after, England had ten thousand soldiers stationed at forts and army bases all around the colonies. These troops were sent here to protect the colonies, and the British didn't really think they should be responsible for buying all the food, ammunition, and supplies that were needed to keep their guys ready to fight.

So around 1764 (the year after the French and Indian War), the king and Parliament in England started passing a bunch of laws saying that the colonists had to pay some taxes to the British Crown. The two big ones were the Sugar Tax and something called the Stamp Act, which said that anytime you wanted to file an official piece of paper with a government office, you needed to buy a stamp for it. Think of it as being like the way you have to buy a postage stamp if you want to mail a letter. The idea was that the colonists would pay a few of these little taxes, and the British would use that money to help keep the colonies safe from the French and the American Indians and the grizzly bears and whatever else the colonists happened to be afraid of at the time.

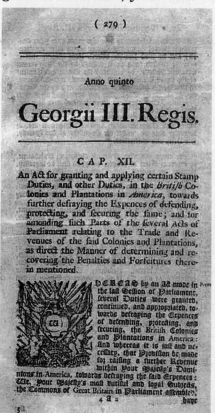

Printed copy of the Stamp Act, 1765

Now, that might not sound like such a big deal. Heck, I have to pay sales tax every time I buy a new Xbox game or a Big Mac.

But for the colonists, this was the sort of thing that made guys start screaming so hard their faces turned the color of a fire truck, because all taxes in the colonies were approved by the British Parliament, and the British Parliament was full of British people. Americans didn't have any representation in the government to stick up for them or negotiate about these taxes.

This made Sam Adams pretty righteously angry, and he was going to make sure every single person in Boston realized that this Stamp Act and Sugar Tax nonsense was the most horrible thing that had ever happened in the history of the civilized world. He started writing letters to newspapers, gave intense pump-up speeches in crowded taverns and meetinghouses, and ran for political office in the Colony of Massachusetts. He was elected to the Massachusetts General Court in 1765 and immediately launched into fiery debates about "no taxation without representation." His demands were clear and not open for discussion: America should either have a vote in the British government, or America should start its own government and be independent of England.

Churches, bars, and other places posted copies of Adams's speeches and declarations. A group called the Sons of Liberty formed chapters throughout the colonies, meeting in bars and taverns from Boston to Charleston to talk about how they were sick and tired of being bossed around by Englishmen. The Stamp Act was supposed to go into effect on November 1, 1765, but the citizens of Boston were totally flipping out and trying to prevent that from happening. Most of the protests were peaceful, but on one particularly violent night in August, a Frankenstein-style mob of angry Bostonians started setting stuff on fire and marched to the home of the lieutenant governor of Massachusetts. He ran for his life, and the mob broke all his windows, trashed his mansion with axes and pitchforks, and set the place on fire.

The Stamp Tax was never actually collected. This was because every person who had been hired to collect the Stamp Tax quit. I guess no job is worth one of your patriotic neighbors trying to smash your house apart with a pitchfork.

This was a pretty good victory for the people who hated King George, but Great Britain didn't build the largest empire in human history by just kicking back and chilling every time one of its colonies got a little rebellious. And it wasn't about to start now. The British responded in the same way they responded to most challenges to their authority—with overwhelming brute force.

With tensions rising in the colonies, the British sent warships into Boston Harbor and unloaded two regiments of the king's best soldiers—nearly four thousand heavily armed combat veterans. These crack infantrymen immediately moved to positions within the city, fixed bayonets on their muskets, and dared anyone to start trouble.

For a while it worked. But then, a few years later, they found some colonists willing to accept the challenge.

On March 5, 1770, a group of British soldiers in their ultra-recognizable bright red uniforms were stationed outside the Old State House in downtown Boston. A large group of Americans, angry that the British Army was all up in their business, started screaming, throwing things at the troops, and telling the Brits to go back home. The British troops, surrounded by angry Bostonians, got a little nervous about the growing number of protestors. In the middle of the chaos, the British soldiers lost their cool, lowered their rifles, and fired straight into the crowd of unarmed protestors at point-blank range.

Over the next minute or so, eight British soldiers ripped two volleys off into the mob. Three Bostonians were killed, including Crispus Attucks, a runaway slave of African-American and Wampanoag Indian descent. Eight more were shot and wounded, and two of those people died of their wounds. To this day, you can go to Boston and stand on the spot where these Colonial patriots lost their lives.

It was our buddy Sam Adams who coined the term *Boston Massacre* to describe the violence on March 5, 1770. Adams was in the Boston State House the very next day, demanding

the immediate removal of British soldiers from Boston. When the governor (the one whose house had just been burned down) gave some lame excuse about how he "didn't have the authority" to order British troops around, Sam Adams unleashed one of the all-time greatest threats ever: "It is at your peril if you refuse. The meeting is composed of three thousand people. They have become impatient. A thousand men are already arrived from the neighborhood, and the whole country is in motion. Night is approaching. An immediate answer is expected."

The governor backed down then and there. The crowd went wild. The British troops that evacuated became known as "Sam Adams' Regiment" throughout Boston, and Sammy became known as the "Iron Man of the People" for his guts in standing up to the governor.

For the next couple of years, the British government kind of chilled out and let things settle down. It moved the soldiers to a fort outside town so they couldn't massacre colonists or anything. They repealed the Stamp Act.

But then, in 1773, things got bad again. The British passed another tax: the Tea Act.

Once again, this was a tax that had been forced on America without any input from the colonies. It's actually a pretty complicated piece of governmental mumbo-jumbo, but here's the short version: The Tea Act placed a big tax on tea, and *then* it said nobody was allowed to buy tea from anyone except the British East India Company. This meant that a lot of American companies were going to go out of business, and that the colonists were going to have to pay a lot of money to a company that was basically run by the guys who were running the British Parliament.

I'll give you one guess as to how well this went over with the colonists.

In Charleston, South Carolina, they stacked the East India Company's boxes of tea on the dock and left them there until they rotted. In New York City and Philadelphia, angry citizens forced the company's ships to turn around and sail right back to England. In Boston, Sam Adams and a few of his buddies organized something a little more dramatic.

On the night of December 16, 1773, an angry mob of colonists, dressed up as American Indians, swarmed aboard the British East India Company ships in Boston Harbor, screaming and yelling and scaring the English crews half to death. The mob of torch-wielding maniacs ransacked the ships, grabbed every crate of tea they could find, and threw every last one into the harbor.

Needless to say, King George III was not amused by the so-called "Boston Tea Party."

The king acted with ruthless efficiency. Warships entered Boston Harbor and shut down all traffic in or out. Troops

swarmed through the streets of Boston, busting up taverns, meetinghouses, and assemblies of the Sons of Liberty.
Bostonians were not allowed to meet in groups. Soldiers were
positioned at the most important street corners, and they
even kicked people out of their homes to make room for the
British soldiers. A set of harsh laws called the Coercive Acts
(and known in the colonies as the Intolerable Acts) were created to punish the people of Boston for failing to appreciate
the authority of the king. Boston was to be treated as a conquered city, and it was going to stay that way until the citizens
paid for every ounce of tea they'd destroyed. With interest.

By the light of a candle in a quiet room, Sam Adams sat
down, picked up his quill, dipped it into a vial of black ink,

and began writing. What came out was considered treason against the British Crown. A crime punishable by death.

He wrote that the time for negotiation and reason was over. He wrote that it was time for action.

By morning, printed copies of his letter, the Solemn League and Covenant, would be posted on every meeting board across New England. Sam Adams and the people of Boston had been looking for a fight, and now they were about to start one for real.

First Blood

The first American killed in the American Revolution was an eleven-year-old boy named Christopher Seider. On February 22, 1770, a big group of patriots in Boston's North End was really angry with a loyalist customs employee named Ebenezer Richardson. So they went to his house and started shouting and throwing rocks at his windows. Ebenezer got angry and fired a gun to try to scare the mob away, but the bullet hit Christopher, killing him. Sam Adams paid for Seider's funeral, and thousands of Bostonians turned out to pay their respects. When the king of England declared that Ebenezer Richardson had committed no crime, the people of Boston got even angrier. The Boston Massacre occurred a little over a week later.

How'd You Come Up with That One?

It was super-illegal to start talking trash about the king of England, so a lot of revolutionary writers used to publish their letters using a fake name called a pen name. One of my all-time favorite pen names is the one used by Sam Adams's cousin, future president of the United States John Adams. When John wrote something bad about the king, he used the fantastic pen name Humphrey Ploughjogger, even though that sounds like it should be the name of one of SpongeBob's friends.

Give Me Liberty

Down south in Virginia, the most vocal anti-taxation politician was a plantation owner named Patrick Henry. Giving impassioned speeches in the Virginia House of Burgesses (a local government that included future US presidents George Washington and Thomas Jefferson), Patrick Henry helped create a bill called the Virginia Resolves. This stated that according to British law, the king could not force the Stamp Act or the Sugar Tax on Virginia, because Virginia did not have any seats in the British Parliament. (Sound familiar?) After Britain clamped the Coercive Acts on Boston, Henry gave one of the most powerful speeches of the Revolution, declaring, "Give me liberty or give me death!"

Know Your Founding Fathers

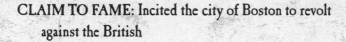

NAME: Samuel Adams

BIRTHDAY: September 27, 1722

BIRTHPLACE: Boston, Massachusetts

CLAIM TO FAME: Incited the city of Boston to revolt against the British

JOB BEFORE THE WAR: Member of the Massachusetts House of Representatives

ROLE IN THE WAR: Member of the Continental Congresses

AFTER THE WAR: Governor of Massachusetts from 1794 to 1797

BONUS FACT: Adams's family owned a malthouse, where they produced malt to make beer and whiskey. Adams tried to help out but failed miserably, losing all his money in the process. Nowadays, Sam Adams has a very famous beer company named after him, even though he was never actually any good at making the stuff.

The Shot Heard Round the World

The Battles of Lexington and Concord
Lexington and Concord, Massachusetts
April 19, 1775

> By the rude bridge that arched the flood,
> Their flag to April's breeze unfurled,
> Here once the embattled farmers stood,
> And fired the shot heard round the world.
>
> —Ralph Waldo Emerson, "Concord Hymn"

JUST BEFORE MIDNIGHT ON APRIL 18, 1775, the commander of all British forces in North America assembled many of his top officers for a secret meeting. By the flickering yellow light of a wax candle, Governor Thomas Gage carefully pointed out locations on a map of Colonial Massachusetts, laying out objectives for the officers who were huddled around his war room table.

Governor Gage was a hardened general in the British Army with over twenty years of experience in the American colonies. He'd survived wars on three continents, personally fought against broadsword-swinging Highlanders in the swamps of Scotland, crossed sabers with ferocious Algonquin warriors in the forests of Quebec, and led bayonet assaults against French fortifications in Belgium. This man was a warrior, and when the king of England tasked him with crushing the early rumblings of rebellion in North America, he had a plan to take care of it.

Under the cover of darkness, the British Tenth Regiment of Foot quietly loaded themselves onto transport ships and began silently sailing across the Charles River toward Charlestown, Massachusetts. From there, orders were to march eighteen miles to the city of Concord, where Gage believed the Americans were putting together a stockpile of cannons, bullets, and equipment for a possible military uprising. Along the way, a few companies of British soldiers were ordered to stop at the town of Lexington and arrest two men on charges of treason: Boston businessman John Hancock and our pal Samuel Adams from chapter 1.

But there was one hitch in their plans: The American patriots had spies everywhere, and they were fantastic at their jobs. As the British ships began making their way across the river, there was a flicker of movement in the highest tower of the tallest building in Boston. Two ordinary lanterns, placed side by side, innocently lit up the steeple of the Old North Church.

While most observers might see this and say, "Okay, cool, someone is up there doing a little late-night reading," the Sons of Liberty knew better. Lanterns in the tower meant one thing and one thing only: *The British are coming*. One lantern would be posted if they were coming by land, two lanterns if they were coming by sea.

The patriots went into action immediately.

Galloping across the countryside on thundering horses, Boston silversmith Paul Revere and his buddy William Dawes hauled tail to warn the colonists that a huge force of British soldiers were on their way to start smashing stuff. Hurtling through the night, Revere and Dawes stopped only to shout their warnings, kicking into gear a network of dozens of riders who charged from Vermont to Connecticut with the news. Sam Adams and John Hancock got their gear and made a break for it. Patriots in Concord began packing up important war materials and either pulled them out of Concord or tried to find good spots in town to hide them in. And all across the countryside, American revolutionary fighters known as minutemen threw on their hats and cartridge boxes and grabbed their rifles.

They were called minutemen because they had to be ready to hop out of bed and fight at a minute's notice. Most of the time they were part of their town's militia, which as

I mentioned earlier is like a neighborhood watch program where everyone is armed to the teeth with rifles and ready to form an army at the drop of a hat. This was a really important thing to have back in a time when a raiding party of American Indians or Frenchmen or armed bandits could come running out of the woods at any moment to try to burn your village down.

The British Army knew these minutemen existed, but you can still imagine their surprise when the soldiers arrived at

The Lexington Minuteman, believed to depict Captain John Parker, sculpted by Henry Hudson Kitson

Lexington on their super–top secret mission to arrest Sam Adams and ended up running dead-on into a group of seventy-seven heavily armed American farmers just outside town.

Dawn was breaking on the morning of April 19, 1775, when the 250 members of the British Tenth Regiment of Foot lined up in battle formation across from the Americans. The detachment's commanding officer, Major John Pitcairn, took one look at this group of gunslinging farmers and was not even a little bit impressed. He was like, "Nice try, dudes," and demanded that the colonists lay down their weapons immediately. The king was the law around these parts, and if this sorry little band of hillbilly yokels didn't like it, they would feel the wrath of the most powerful military force the world had ever seen.

American militia commander Captain John Parker looked at the imposing red wall of hardened British infantry and knew this was a battle he had absolutely no chance of winning. Still, staring down the British formation, Parker allegedly said to his men, "Stand your ground. Don't fire unless fired upon, but if they mean to have a war, let it begin here."

For a moment, all was quiet.

It was at this point that a single gunshot rang out across the field like the bell that kicks off a boxing match.

It was a shot that would change the course of history forever.

Nobody really knows for sure who fired the "Shot Heard

Round the World" or even which direction the bullet came from. It seems highly unlikely that a British Army rifleman would fire his weapon without receiving an order to do so, so my best guess is that it was a colonist who was cranky about the idea of backing down to the redcoats. Honestly, it doesn't matter, because total insanity broke out as soon as that bullet was fired. The minutemen scrambled into cover behind an old stone wall and immediately started firing their muskets. The British commanders ordered "volley fire," which is where every dude in the company stands shoulder-to-shoulder and rips off a bullet the moment they get the order to "ready... aim...*fire!*"

The Battle of Lexington didn't last long. The British cranked off a few volleys, the minutemen tried to return fire, but there was no hope. The Americans fled the field, leaving behind eight men dead and nine more wounded. The British suffered one wounded and lost no one. They searched for Adams, heard he was halfway to Philadelphia, then headed on to meet up with the rest of the Tenth Regiment in Concord.

As the British troops moved through the countryside, though, they kept hearing the ominous sound of alarm bells. By the time they arrived at Concord, nearly four hundred minutemen were assembled in the hills outside town, silently watching their movements.

The Brits stormed into Concord and went to work

completing their mission to smash all the cool stuff the patriots were hiding there. They set fire to wagons, threw a bunch
of gunpowder into the lake, confiscated bullets, and sent soldiers into homes to search for contraband. (In one particularly awesome case, an old Colonial woman slapped a British
major in the face for coming into her home without permission.) Then all twenty-five hundred soldiers (they had gained
some reinforcements by this point) ate lunch and started
their march back to Boston.

This is when things really got rough for them. Because by
this point the forest surrounding the main road leading from
Concord to Boston was almost completely lined with minuteman snipers waiting to ambush the exhausted redcoats.

According to Lieutenant Colonel Francis Smith of the
Tenth Regiment of Foot, for the next eighteen miles (and
eighteen miles is a *long* way to walk!) there were barely five
minutes total in which the redcoats weren't getting shot at
by Colonial troops hiding in the woods along the road. The
Brits did what they could to fight back, but they were wearing bright red uniforms, making them really easy targets for
Colonial marksmen on their home turf.

Probably the greatest story from this part of the battle
is the tale of Captain Samuel Whittemore. Whittemore was
born in England in 1695, and he'd served in the British Army
for over fifty years. But he had taken a liking to the colonies
and was firmly on the side of American freedom. Whittemore,

all alone, with no backup, positioned himself behind a stone wall, waited in ambush for the British soldiers, and then single-handedly engaged an entire British regiment with nothing more than his musket, a pair of dueling pistols, an old French sword, and the pure liquid anger coursing through his veins.

This guy popped up like an old rifle-toting jack-in-the-box the moment the British troops were on top of him. He fired his musket at point-blank range, busting the nearest guy so hard it nearly blew his red coat into the next dimension. Then, with a company of Brits bearing down on him, he quick-drew a matched set of twin flintlock pistols and sent another two redcoats down. *Then* he unsheathed an ornate French sword he'd captured off an enemy officer during King George's War way back in 1748, and this eighty-year-old madman stood his ground in hand-to-hand combat against a couple dozen trained soldiers—each of whom was probably a quarter of his age.

The hand-to-hand didn't work out so well. Whittemore was shot through the face by a .69-caliber bullet, hit with a rifle, and bayonetted thirteen times. The Brits left him for dead and continued their march back to base, harassed the entire way by Whittemore's fellow militiamen.

Amazingly, however, Samuel Whittemore didn't die. When his friends rushed out from their homes to check on his body, they found the half-dead, ultra-bloody eighty-year-old still trying to reload his weapon. The dude actually survived the war, finally dying in 1793 at ninety-eight from old age and awesomeness. A 2005 act of the Massachusetts Legislature declared him an official state hero, and today there's a really cool historical marker at the spot where he made his stand.

All told, about 250 British men were killed or wounded on their daylong death march across the Massachusetts countryside. That night, more American minutemen mobilized and flocked toward the British in Boston. By the following dawn, roughly fifteen thousand Americans had surrounded the small British force holed up inside the city.

The American Revolution had officially begun.

> ...I can't think but it must have been a
> preconcerted scheme in them to attack the
> King's troops the first favourable opportunity
> that offered, otherwise, I think they could not,
> in so short a time as from our marching out, have
> raised such a numerous body, and for so great a
> space of ground.
>
> —Lieutenant Colonel Francis Smith,
> Tenth Regiment of Foot
> Letter to General Thomas Gage,
> April 22, 1775

PATRIOTS AND LOYALISTS

Many people in the America of 1775 had been born in England, had fought on England's side in wars, or just loved the king and the mother country and didn't want to break away. These people didn't like a bunch of rebels taking over their towns, beating up all the redcoats, and setting up a strange system of government that didn't have any logical order (in the loyalists' minds). For these reasons, in the early days of the war, most of the people in the American colonies were either Whigs or patriots (people who supported rebellion) or Tories or loyalists (people who supported staying with England). Each group accused the other of being traitors, and their arguments turned entire cities against one another. Some of the most brutal, cutthroat fighting of the American Revolution occurred not between British and American armies, but between patriot and loyalist military regiments.

WHAT ARE YOU TRYING TO FAY?

When you read letters that were sent during the time of the Revolution, it can be really confusing. If a lowercase letter *s* appears at the beginning or in the middle of a word, it is written as an *f*. So, for instance, *Pursuit of Happiness* becomes *Purfuit of Happinefs*. Also, the People capitalized every Noun in a Sentence (as I am doing in this Sentence), which can make it really difficult for a Person like Me to read.

The Soldiers

The men who fought in the American Revolution came from all walks of life. Some were rich, some were poor; many were young, others were old. They were husbands, fathers, sons, and brothers, all with families waiting for them back home if they were one of the lucky few to make it through the struggle. War is a bloody, terrible thing that pulls families apart and pushes people to the absolute limit of what a human being can take. So let's talk a little bit about what these guys might have been like.

THE AMERICAN SOLDIER

Many of the rebels were using guns they'd brought from home. These could be old shotguns, hunting rifles, captured British rifles, or other weapons that were oftentimes outdated. Many carried a weapon called the Pennsylvania rifle, a long-barreled, muzzle-loading flintlock. It had grooves in the barrel that were designed to spin the bullet, kind of like how you throw a football in a spiral to make it go straighter and not wobble all over the place. These rifles were excellent for hunting because they had great range and were very accurate, but they took a long time to load, and they couldn't mount a bayonet.

The American rebels were dressed in their regular, everyday clothes, typically a three-cornered hat, a long wool coat that hung down to about their knees, a cotton shirt, knee-length breeches, tall white kneesocks, and black shoes with big buckles on them. The style of the day was long hair, usually pulled back into a ponytail, and most men shaved their face regularly. Later in the war, they started importing blue uniforms from France, and they were equipped with the French infantry musket, a big, heavy, inaccurate .69-caliber gun known as the Charleville.

The Americans were typically English colonists, although there were many others of German, Dutch, Polish, Irish, Scottish, and other descent as well. Most of them were wilderness people, used to hunting and shooting in the woods for food or furs, and they could draw detailed maps of the land from memory. Although most settlers had some familiarity with fighting against American

AMERICAN SOLDIER

Indian raids, they had little experience in organized warfare. But they were tough people, hardened by a difficult frontier lifestyle and inspired by their cause. In most cases, they were fighting in their own backyards, defending their homes and their country in a struggle for freedom.

THE BRITISH SOLDIER

The average British soldier was between twenty and forty-five years old, and soldiers were required to stand at least five feet seven inches tall. Enlisted troops, dressed in their scarlet coats, typically came from poor families in Scotland, Wales, England, and Ireland. Their officers typically came from the aristocratic class, because back in those days it was possible to pay money to the army to become an officer. (So if your dad was rich, you could fork over some gold and enlist in the army as a lieutenant or something, even if you had no idea what the heck you were doing. It's like buying premium DLC in *Call of Duty*.) It's estimated that about 60 percent of the British officers in the war bought their rank. A lot of these guys wore those fake white powdered wigs, because they thought the white hair made them look older and more distinguished, and thus more likely to get promoted.

British soldiers carried about sixty pounds of gear, from backpacks and food to ammunition pouches and musket cartridges. They were armed with the Brown Bess, a large, smooth-bore .71-caliber musket that was much heavier and less accurate than the Pennsylvania rifle. But it fired a huge, destructive musket ball. One mega-advantage for these troops was that every British soldier carried a bayonet—a foot-long pointy metal spike that fitted on the end of his rifle and turned it into a gigantic spear—and all soldiers were trained in how to fight in formation with one of those suckers.

Since guns in those days took thirty to forty seconds to reload, the British would march in formation until they were about fifty yards away from the enemy, fire two or three volleys, and then just run in and start stabbing everything. As I said earlier, the Americans' Pennsylvania rifle couldn't hold a bayonet (and there were not many bayonets available to the Americans anyway), so in hand-to-hand combat the British had a massive advantage. The saying was that the British would "pray for rain" before a battle with the Colonials...

BRITISH SOLDIER

because muskets at this time wouldn't fire if their gun-powder got too wet. So any fight in a rainstorm was usu-ally decided with the bayonet rather than with gunfire. After just a few encounters, the Americans quickly came to fear British bayonets almost as much as they feared British cannons.

Know Your Founding Fathers

NAME: John Hancock

BIRTHDAY: January 23, 1737

BIRTHPLACE: Braintree, Massachusetts

CLAIM TO FAME: Has the biggest signature on the
Declaration of Independence

JOB BEFORE THE WAR: Merchant ship owner and politician

ROLE IN THE WAR: President of the Second Continental
Congress

AFTER THE WAR: Governor of Massachusetts from 1780 to
1785 and from 1787 to 1793

BONUS FACT: Hancock's dad was a minister, but he died
when John was just seven years old, so John was adopted
and raised by his uncle and aunt.

Bunker Hill

England Learns What It's Dealing With

Charlestown, Massachusetts
June 17, 1775

> Powder is scarce and must not be wasted. Do not fire until you see the whites of their eyes.
>
> —Colonel William Prescott, Massachusetts Militia

S O WHAT HAD BEEN A COUPLE OF GRUMPY loudmouths complaining about taxes was now a full-blown shooting rebellion against the British Empire. The British Army was barricaded inside Boston, with nearly fifteen thousand angry Massachusetts colonists surrounding the city, and more disgruntled Americans were arriving daily to show their discontent at gunpoint.

The British weren't trapped by any means—Boston Harbor

was filled with Royal Navy warships that could sail in and out of the city at will. But all that changed in April 1775 when a group of rebel militiamen known as the Green Mountain Boys (honestly, that sounds more like a terrible band name than a military company) captured Fort Ticonderoga at the northern tip of New York. Ticonderoga wasn't a particularly exciting place, and there wasn't a huge British garrison there, but it did have something that put a little bit of fear into the hearts of the British Army in Boston.

Cannons. Big ones. A lot of them.

It was going to take quite a bit of time to drag those cannons all the way across Massachusetts, but the British Army still had to act quickly. Governor Thomas Gage knew that there were really only two good places the Americans could put cannons if they wanted to shell Boston: the Dorchester Heights to the south, and the Charlestown Peninsula to the north. If American cannons were set up at either position, it would mean big trouble for the British dudes living in Boston.

We'll never know how the American spies figured out that Governor Gage was planning to capture Charlestown. It's one of those stories that is probably super-exciting, super-interesting James Bond, *Assassin's Creed* kind of stuff, but it went down on the super-secret. All we know for sure is that some brave patriot came running out to the American lines on the night of June 16, 1775, and he told the rebel leadership that the British were planning to seize Charlestown.

The Americans had to act fast. So, in the middle of the night, they tapped two of their most experienced commanders and a few hardworking minutemen to grab that position first.

Colonel William Prescott of the Massachusetts Militia was a hardened veteran who had fought bravely in the French and Indian War. Prescott was probably a little bitter that he'd missed the opportunity to take potshots at the redcoats during the Concord battles. So as soon as he heard there might be the chance for a fight, he put together a group of one thousand strong men, told them to grab their shovels, picks, and rifles, and hauled out.

Now, there are two big hills on the Charlestown Peninsula. The bigger one is called Bunker Hill, and that's the one Prescott was supposed to secure. The smaller one is called Breed's Hill, and *that's* the one Prescott actually built a fort on. We don't know whether he was just brave, or bad at geography, or what. But it's caused a lot of problems for people who study history over the years, because the famous Battle of Bunker Hill was actually fought on Breed's Hill, which is very confusing. You can't open a history book without reading this fact, because historians love silly little details like that (and anything else that makes us feel like we're smarter than everyone else).

Anyway, in the dead of night on June 16, 1775, William Prescott and a thousand gunslinging farmers climbed up Breed's Hill on the Charlestown Peninsula and built an awesome fort. They worked all night long planting pointed stakes, digging holes they could use for cover, and building a wooden fence they could hide behind while they shot at the British. You can be pretty sure that when the sun came up on June 17, the British were a little surprised.

The first Brits to see the fort were the crew of the HMS *Lively*, a warship sitting in the river that separated Charlestown from Boston. The crew of the *Lively* was so mad that they immediately started shooting their cannons at the fort. It wasn't long before the other gunships in the harbor started firing as well. Most of the shots missed, but two cannonballs found their mark: One blew up the barrel where Prescott's men stored their fresh water, and the other actually knocked an American guy's head off.

You can probably imagine what it might have been like to be sitting at the top of the hill that morning. These guys were woken up in the middle of the night, walked a mile or two up a hill, and spent twelve hours digging a bunch of holes in the ground, and now they were hungry and exhausted and had no clean water to drink. Even worse, six British warships were using them for target practice, and some dude's head had just popped off, which is pretty scary if you ask me.

One guy who didn't seem to have a problem with any of

this was Colonel William Prescott. As bullets and cannonballs whizzed past his head, Prescott calmly walked up and down the American fortifications like he was strolling through the mall on a Saturday morning. When he saw an American militiaman who looked freaked out, Prescott would stop, tell him a joke, and then talk to the guy until he chilled out a little. "Don't worry, bud. We got this."

Back in Boston, the British Army assembled and made plans to crush these good-for-nothing rebels with a show of force that would make the Death Star look like a Nerf basketball. Governor Gage appointed Major General William Howe to lead the attack. Howe had been in the British Army for twenty-nine years, serving on battlefields from Belgium to Quebec, and this guy had absolutely no respect for these disorganized American farmers. One of his junior officers, General Johnny Burgoyne (we'll meet him later on when we talk about Saratoga), once wrote that government authority "depends in a great measure upon the idea that trained troops are invincible against any numbers or any position of untrained rabble." And Howe believed that there was no band of yokels in existence who stood a chance against the greatest professional army on the planet.

Howe loaded twenty-two hundred redcoats into rowboats, sailed across the Charles River, and unloaded his troops at the bottom of Breed's Hill. Then he ordered the guys to sit down and eat lunch. This made the Americans atop Breed's Hill even more bummed out that they didn't have anything to eat, but it also bought the colonists time to bring up some reinforcements. Militias from Connecticut and New Hampshire took up positions to protect the flank (side) of Prescott's line and keep the British from swinging around the back.

At three PM on June 17, 1775, the invincible British Army lined up in battle formation, shoulder-to-shoulder, and prepared to crush the rebellion with one decisive strike. The

Battle of Bunker Hill, painted by E. Percy Moran

soldiers attached bayonets to the ends of their rifles, and the sun glinted off their weaponry as they assembled for war. They were dressed in bright red coats, with big black bearskin hats, white pants, and black boots that marched in unison to the beat of their war drums. Large banners and British flags flapped in the wind as they began a steady, unstoppable march up the hill.

At the top of Breed's Hill, William Prescott's men were starting to get a little nervous. Remember, these guys were poorly trained farmers, and most of them had never even been in a battle before. They didn't have uniforms. They didn't have bayonets. They were using old rifles they'd brought from home. They hadn't slept in over a day. These minutemen weren't expecting to have to fight a battle, and a lot of these guys hadn't even brought enough powder to shoot their guns more than five or six times. Now they were being asked to defend a hill against the army of the largest empire in human history.

Once again, William Prescott made his way up and down the American lines. His voice was calm but dead serious. He told his men: "Be brave, be strong, and don't shoot until you are absolutely certain you can hit an enemy. Aim for the officers first, and aim low so that you take out their legs." The quote that became famous from this battle is "Don't fire until you see the whites of their eyes," although a lot of argumentative historians like to complain that this is just an awesome story and Prescott didn't really say it. Honestly, it doesn't matter. The point is that he told his men to wait until the enemy was fifty yards away...*and don't miss.*

Now, the British plan of charging uphill into a group of fortified enemy infantry is pretty much a terrible idea, but that was kind of the point. William Howe had no respect for the American fighters, and he was absolutely convinced that the colonists were going to pee their pants and run away as soon as the British Army got close enough to fire.

Unfortunately for him, it didn't go down that way.

When the redcoats were within fifty yards of the American lines, a huge ripple of white gun smoke puffed out from the patriots' rifles. Less than a second later, the zip of musket balls cracked and ripped straight through the British lines, slamming into men and sending dozens of soldiers spinning to the ground. The entire front rank of the redcoats was shattered with one blast of gunfire, and the British were so unprepared for this that they immediately pulled back in disarray, retreating down the hill as the American forces cheered. At the base of the hill, the British re-formed, attacked again, and met the same fate: a murderous hail of close-range gunfire that claimed the lives of hundreds of soldiers.

Now the British were mad. They rolled up cannons. They called in reinforcements, rowing four hundred Royal Marines across the river to join the attack. British gunboats launched burning-hot cannonballs into the town of Charlestown, setting the city on fire to root out the

American snipers hiding in the buildings. At the bottom of the hill, the redcoats once again fixed bayonets, resolving to capture this hill or die trying.

The third attack on Breed's Hill took place late in the afternoon. It was personally led by Lieutenant Colonel Sir Robert Pigot, an ultra-brave warrior who was also a sitting Member of Parliament...meaning that this was basically the British equivalent of a current US senator leading a bayonet charge. Pigot ordered his men forward, again with the drums and flags and lockstep precision, and this time the British were ready for what awaited them. As Pigot charged up the hill, bayonets and rifles at the ready, another group under General Howe went up the hill from a different direction, trying to swing around behind the rebels.

Once again, Prescott ordered his men to hold their fire. It was a hot day, these men were exhausted, and their ammunition was almost gone. They were going to get one shot, and then they'd be fighting for their lives in hand-to-hand combat.

When the British attack was basically right on top of the Americans, Prescott gave the order to fire. Yet again, a shock wave of musket fire blasted through the British lines, but this time the redcoats didn't break. They kept their formation, broke into a run, lowered their bayonets, and jumped over the earthworks spear-first into the American forces.

One Royal Marine later wrote: "Nothing could be more shocking than the carnage that followed the storming of this

work." In a huge swirling fight that more closely resembled a battle scene from *The Lord of the Rings* than anything you'd expect from the American Revolution, the British and American soldiers pounded, stabbed, bit, kicked, punched, and fought with everything they had. Guys were climbing over dead and wounded men, leaping over trenches, shooting with pistols, and swinging their rifles like baseball bats. Prescott's men, outnumbered and without the advantage of bayonets, were getting the worst of it, and Prescott soon ordered them to retreat. As his men fell back, they saw Prescott, standing atop the hill with a sword drawn, personally fighting off a group of three rifle-swinging Brits.

The British captured Breed's Hill and drove the Americans off the Charlestown Heights, but at a staggering cost. Of the twenty-two hundred men they'd sent up the hill, half of them were dead or wounded. One hundred officers were dead. When word reached England, everyone was shocked and horrified by the losses the British Army had suffered. The king himself was furious. He issued a Proclamation of Rebellion, ordering all people loyal to the king to bring justice to "the authors, perpetrators, and abetters of such traitorous designs."

As for the Americans, even though they'd lost the hill, they were bolstered by the idea that this was a fight they actually had a chance of winning. As patriot leader Nathanael Greene so eloquently put it, "I wish we could sell them another hill at the same price."

Proclamation of Rebellion

King George III
August 23, 1775

Whereas many of our subjects in divers parts of our Colonies and Plantations in North America, misled by dangerous and ill designing men, and forgetting the allegiance which they owe to the power that has protected and sustained them; after various disorderly acts committed in disturbance of the publick peace, to the obstruction of lawful commerce, and to the oppression of our loyal subjects carrying on the same; have at length proceeded to an open and avowed rebellion, by arraying themselves in hostile manner, to withstand the execution of the law, and traitorously preparing, ordering and levying war against us: And whereas, there is reason to apprehend that such rebellion hath been much promoted and encouraged by the traitorous correspondence, counsels and comfort of divers wicked and desperate persons within this Realm: To the end therefore, that none of our subjects may neglect or violate their duty through ignorance thereof, or through any doubt of the protection which the law will afford to their loyalty and zeal, we have thought fit, by and with the advice of our Privy Council, to issue this our Royal Proclamation, hereby declaring, that not only all our Officers, civil and military, are obliged to exert their utmost endeavours to suppress such rebellion, and to bring the traitors to justice, but that all our subjects of this Realm, and the dominions thereunto belonging, are bound by law to be aiding and assisting in the suppression of such rebellion, and to disclose and make known all traitorous conspiracies and attempts against us, our crown and dignity; and we do accordingly strictly charge and command all our Officers, as well civil as military, and all other our obedient and loyal subjects, to use their utmost endeavours to withstand and suppress such rebellion, and to disclose and make known all treasons and traitorous conspiracies which they shall know to be against us, our crown and dignity; and for that purpose, that they transmit to one of our principal Secretaries of State, or other proper officer, due and full information of all persons who shall be found carrying on correspondence with, or in any manner or degree aiding or abetting the persons now in open arms and rebellion against our Government, within any of our Colonies and Plantations in North America, in order to bring to condign punishment the authors, perpetrators, and abetters of such traitorous designs.

Given at our Court at St. James's the twenty-third day of August, one thousand seven hundred and seventy-five, in the fifteenth year of our reign.

GOD save the KING.

AT LEAST THEY BUILT IT ON THE RIGHT HILL

Nowadays there is a 221-foot-tall stone obelisk atop Breed's Hill commemorating the Battle of Bunker Hill. The Marquis de Lafayette (more about him in chapter 9) laid the cornerstone in 1825, but the project ran out of money after they'd built only half of the tower. So in 1843, a magazine editor named Sarah Josepha Hale (the woman credited with writing the song "Mary Had a Little Lamb") had a week-long bake sale, and the women of Boston were able to raise enough money to complete the project. To this day, members of the Boston Fire Department train by climbing the 294 steps to the top of the monument while wearing sixty pounds of firefighting gear. Which sounds like quite a workout. But at least these guys don't have anybody shooting at them like the British did when they tried to huff sixty pounds of gear up Breed's Hill.

CAN'T IT WAIT UNTIL MORNING?

Remember when I talked about the Green Mountain Boys capturing Fort Ticonderoga? Well, the battle itself wasn't quite as exciting as you might think. All that really happened was that the British commander heard screaming and guys banging swords together, and he was so surprised and freaked out that he ran outside in his pajamas and surrendered immediately.

Know Your Founding Fathers

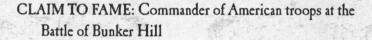

NAME: William Prescott

BIRTHDAY: February 20, 1726

BIRTHPLACE: Groton, Massachusetts

CLAIM TO FAME: Commander of American troops at the Battle of Bunker Hill

JOB BEFORE THE WAR: Provincial British Army militia commander

ROLE IN THE WAR: Colonel in the Massachusetts Militia

AFTER THE WAR: Commanded troops that suppressed Shays' Rebellion in 1786; served in the Massachusetts General Court

BONUS FACT: His grandson, William Hickling Prescott, is a famous historian who wrote a number of books about the early history of Spain in North America. He also married the granddaughter of John Linzee, the captain of the HMS *Falcon*—one of the British warships that fired on the American troops at Bunker Hill.

Building the Continental Army

The Second Continental Congress and the Siege of Boston

Philadelphia, Pennsylvania, Upstate New York, and Boston, Massachusetts May 10, 1775–March 17, 1776

> We have too many high sounding words, and too few actions that correspond with them.
>
> —Abigail Adams

NOTORIOUS "ENEMIES OF THE CROWN" Sam Adams and John Hancock had barely avoided having their heads twisted off by British soldiers at Lexington, Massachusetts, and now they were on the move, riding hard on horseback through the countryside. Traveling day and night for hundreds of miles, the two patriots headed south to the large metropolis of Philadelphia, Pennsylvania. There, in the heart of the bustling city, the outlaws moved through crowds of people and horses and finally approached the Pennsylvania State House—a tall brick building that was suddenly the command center of the American Colonial rebellion. Within the great hall of the State House sat a large group of powerful, influential men assembled from all thirteen colonies in America. With somber faces and funny-looking white powdered wigs, these rebel political leaders joined together to discuss one simple question:

What the heck was America going to do now that they'd really ticked off the king of England?

While it might seem pretty clear to you and me what direction this story is going in, in May 1775 this wasn't exactly an easy question to answer. Here were the facts: American militiamen had opened fire on British soldiers and had killed a bunch of them, and a big mob of New England militiamen were laying siege to the British garrison at Boston. The king of England had declared that all rebels were traitors and should be put to death, and it was only a matter of time before he was going to send reinforcements across the Atlantic and start smashing everything in America.

Now this assembly, known as the Second Continental Congress, had to decide how to deal with the facts.

As with everything else that involves government, there was a lot of arguing, debate, and discussion. One of the loudest voices in the room was that of Sam Adams's cousin, a well-known Boston lawyer named John Adams. He laid out a bold proposal: We need to declare that the New England militia troops outside Boston are not an Army of Massachusetts but an American army representing thirteen colonies united in rebellion against King George III and the United Kingdom.

Now all they needed was a guy to lead it.

Well, so far all the fighting had taken place outside Boston, and a lot of people thought John Adams would just nominate a Massachusetts guy to command the Continental Army. Like General Artemas Ward, the man who was in charge up there. But John Adams knew that Boston wasn't alone in its struggle. The Virginia government had openly written letters defying the king's unjust taxes (remember the Virginia Resolves from earlier?). Charleston, South Carolina, had sealed its ports against British imports. North Carolina towns had patriots and loyalists fighting each other in the streets. Vermonters had captured Fort Ticonderoga in New York. This was a wide-ranging American Revolution, and it needed to be led by a man who represented not just Boston, but all the colonies.

On June 15, 1775, after two long days of debate, Continental Congress president John Hancock officially assigned the position of army commander in chief to a soldier from Virginia named George Washington.

I'm going to go out on a limb here and guess that you've probably heard this name before.

George Washington was born on February 22, 1732, in Westmoreland County, Virginia. He was exceptionally tall, and he had such a dominant personality that every time he stepped into a room everyone stopped and took notice. Dressed in a long military officer's coat and tall black boots, George Washington was an imposing, powerful man who looked like something out of a real-life superhero movie. He had fired the first shots of the French and Indian War in 1754, and a few months later he was commended for bravery when he saved his unit from annihilation during a failed British attack on a French fortress. By the end of the French and Indian War, Lieutenant Colonel George Washington was leading the defense of Virginia and was the highest-ranking officer in the Colonial military. He'd spent sixteen years in the Virginia Colonial government and had represented his state in the First and Second Continental Congresses.

Now the forty-three-year-old colonel was facing the most imposing challenge of his life: Take a group of untrained farmer rebels and forge them into a hammer capable of taking on the most powerful military in the world.

On July 3, 1775, General George Washington arrived outside Boston and assumed command of the Continental Army. Now, here's something to keep in mind when we talk about Washington: He wasn't chosen because he was a military genius, capable of outmaneuvering and destroying his enemies left and right with godlike precision. Heck, before taking command of the Continental Army, this guy had lost the only two major battles he'd ever fought. He was chosen because he was a *leader*, a man who was determined, dedicated, and respected. A guy who could take a huge, diverse group of untrained farmers with no experience or equipment and make them into a force that could fight for freedom.

It must have been a crazy sight outside Boston in 1775. In addition to mobs of disorganized minutemen, there was the Twenty-First Massachusetts Regiment, a group of salty sailors and fishermen who had gone to war after King George established the Fisheries Act, which was a lot like the Stamp Act and ruined their town financially. There was Stark's First New Hampshire Regiment, in matching blue coats with black three-cornered hats, and Ritzema's Third New York, a force of Dutch and German immigrants in gray uniforms. The Rhode Island Brigade was there, under handsome young Nathanael Greene, as well as a hardened Connecticut militia group under scarred-up American Indian fighter Israel Putnam. There was everything from steely veterans to untrained farmers, from every part of the country, all together with no real leadership to speak of. Imagine getting Jets, Patriots, Bills, Giants, and Eagles fans to all agree on something and you'll have a basic idea of what Washington was working with in Boston.

He got his hands dirty immediately. Washington organized his army into cohesive units, trained them, appointed officers, and set up supplies and logistics. He had horsemen gallop off all through the American countryside to rally more men to the cause. He issued a call not just for warriors, but also for gunsmiths, horsemen, shoemakers, wagoneers, cooks, farmers, and anyone else who might be able to help keep an army functioning.

He had about fifteen thousand men surrounding Boston, where ten thousand British were holed up along with a few thousand civilians. The British had their navy in the harbor and had control of Bunker Hill, but Washington still had the option of the Dorchester Heights, which would be a perfect spot to set up cannons to rain destruction onto the British. But to succeed, he was going to need a little help.

At some point after Washington took command, he was approached by an overweight twenty-five-year-old Boston bookstore owner named Henry Knox. Knox had personally witnessed the Boston Massacre and had fought as a rifleman at the Battle of Bunker Hill. But this guy's expertise was that he was totally obsessed with cannons. He'd never actually *fired* a cannon in real life, sure, but he knew everything you could possibly know from reading a book. This made him, by default, the most experienced artilleryman in the Continental Army. So (partly at the request of Samuel Adams, a good friend of Henry Knox's) George Washington made him a colonel and put him in charge of the artillery arm of the Continental Army.

Of course, there was one minor problem.

The only artillery the Continental Army had access to were those guns sitting three hundred miles away at Fort Ticonderoga.

No problem. Knox knew how to get things done. He rode the three hundred miles from Boston to New York to check out Fort Ticonderoga and its graveyard of busted cannons. Most of them were unusable, but Knox found fifty-nine guns ranging from four-pounders to twenty-four-pounders that could be salvaged. All he had to do was drag them three hundred miles back to Boston across unpaved roads through snow and ice in the middle of December, and he'd have to be quiet about it because he didn't have any infantry to defend the convoy. If the British figured out what was going down, they'd roll up and turn the entire column of men and cannons into a mile-long line of corpses.

Knox found forty-two sledges (big sleds) and recruited an army of civilian workers, horses, oxen, and donkeys. When the guns needed to go up a steep hill, all the guys in the convoy pushed them like they were cars that had gotten stuck in the snow. When they needed to go downhill, Knox's men

used chains and ropes to slowly lower them. When a couple
of cannons broke through a layer of ice while being dragged
across a frozen lake, Knox engineered a team to ice-fish them
out of there.

This epic journey took around three months. When
Washington saw Knox arriving at the head of the convoy, he
almost couldn't believe it.

On the night of March 4, 1776, the Continental Army
dragged fifty cannons up to the Dorchester Heights and dug
an impressive network of defenses around them. The British
woke up in Boston on March 5, saw a bunch of gun barrels

**Ox teams hauling guns from Fort Ticonderoga
for the siege of Boston**

pointed at them, and got really nervous. British general William Howe thought about trying to charge the guns, but Washington had a force of three thousand guys lined up and ready to storm Boston if the British left it undefended. Howe wrote a letter to Washington with a deal: "If you let us get into our boats and sail out of town, I promise I won't burn Boston to the ground."

Washington agreed. And on March 17, 1776, British soldiers and loyalist colonists boarded ships in Boston Harbor and set sail north to Canada to regroup.

Colonel Henry Knox led the way into the city, and by the end of the day the flag of the American colonies was flying over the city of Boston. George Washington had his first military victory over the British, and the Continental Army was starting to show its teeth.

THE SEQUEL WAS BETTER

The First Continental Congress was formed right after the British passed the Coercive Acts in 1775 (these were called the Intolerable Acts by the Americans, and you can read a little more about them back in chapter 1). This Congress met for seven weeks, had fifty-six delegates who came from every colony except Georgia, and decided that the colonies were going to refuse all British imports until the Coercive Acts were repealed. Honestly, it wasn't that exciting. The second one is the important one.

THE BATTLE OF CHARLESTON

Most of the early fighting in the war took place in the northern colonies, but there was plenty of action in the southern colonies as well. On June 28, 1776, a fleet of nine British warships approached Charleston, South Carolina, preparing to drop off more than two thousand redcoat soldiers. A small group of Colonial soldiers on one of the islands in Charleston Harbor was all that opposed them. Colonel William Moultrie's Second Carolina Infantry laid into the British invasion force with everything it had. Moultrie ordered his gunners to fire "chain shot," which is when you tie two cannonballs together with a big chain and then fire them both out of the gun at the same time. The chain shot ripped through the mast of one of the British ships, and another literally blew the pants off the British admiral (which is hilarious). The Brits tried to send their gunboats around to attack Moultrie from a different side, but those ships ran aground. Defeated, humiliated, and pantsless, the British gave up their invasion. They wouldn't return to Charleston for another four years.

THOSE STUBBORN FLORIDIANS

Florida was a British colony at the time of the American Revolution, and the only one that never even considered joining the American cause. British bases in Florida such as Pensacola and Saint Augustine were used as staging points for attacks into Georgia during the war, and stayed loyal to the Crown until Florida was captured by Spain in 1779. They didn't give it back to England until after the war.

Flags of the War

Flags played a very important role in the Revolutionary War, especially since this was a time when basically every army unit marched into battle with a couple of flags fluttering proudly over its formation. Flags helped inspire morale and showed men where their units were, and you could usually tell how bad you were winning or losing by looking across the field and seeing where everyone's flags were. Here's a rundown of a few of the most important flags of the American Revolution:

DON'T TREAD ON ME

Designed by South Carolina general Christopher Gadsden, this flag features a coiled rattlesnake on a yellow field and just says DON'T TREAD ON ME. It's a reference to an old political cartoon drawn by Benjamin Franklin in 1754, when Franklin wrote the phrase JOIN, OR DIE below a rattlesnake that had been cut into thirteen pieces. Each piece represented one of the thirteen colonies. Late in 1775, when the war began, Gadsden was telling the British, "Yeah, we joined, now you're gonna die."

THE UNION JACK

The British flag is pretty much the same today as it was during the Revolution, except for one small difference. When the United Kingdom officially changed its name to the United Kingdom of Great Britain and Ireland in 1801, it added a little red X (the Cross of Saint Patrick) over the white X on its flag. Those red lines weren't there in 1776.

THE GRAND UNION FLAG

The first flag of the united colonies was the Grand Union Flag, which looks a lot like the current American flag, except it has a British Union Jack in the top left corner instead of the fifty stars we know today. The Grand Union Flag is believed to have been first stitched by a Philadelphia hatmaker named Margaret Manny, and it was the official flag of the colonies until 1777.

THE BETSY ROSS FLAG

 On June 14, 1777, the Second Continental Congress approved a change to the Grand Union Flag that replaced the Union Jack with a circle of thirteen stars, each one representing a colony. This flag bears the name of the first woman who stitched it a year earlier, twenty-four-year-old Philadelphia seamstress Betsy Ross. Today we celebrate Flag Day on June 14 every year. Yeah, you didn't realize that Flag Day was a for-real holiday, did you? Well, now you know.

THE FRENCH FLAG

 The modern blue, white, and red French flag didn't exist until after the French Revolution in 1789—and they totally copied the United States and based their colors on the colors of the American flag. During the American Revolution, the French flag was actually the flag of the royal House of Bourbon, where the kings of France (and also King Carlos of Spain) came from. It was made up of a bunch of gold fleur-de-lis (pronounced

fler-deh-*lee*), those little flower things you see on the New Orleans Saints football helmets, on a white background.

REGIMENTAL FLAGS

Many regiments in the British and Colonial armies had their own special flags, custom-made. Some were pretty simple designs, while others were incredibly ornate, with pictures; stars and other symbols; phrases; and names of battles where the regiment had fought. These flags were often hand-stitched by the wives, sisters, mothers, and neighbors of the regiment's soldiers, and one of the worst things that could possibly happen to a unit was to have its "colors" (flag) captured by the enemy during a battle.

Know Your Founding Fathers

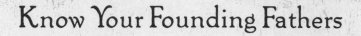

NAME: George Washington

BIRTHDAY: February 22, 1732

BIRTHPLACE: Westmoreland County, Virginia

CLAIM TO FAME: Commander of American forces in the Revolution

JOB BEFORE THE WAR: Politician, plantation owner, lieutenant colonel in the Virginia Militia

ROLE IN THE WAR: Overall commander of all American forces

AFTER THE WAR: First president of the United States, serving from 1789 to 1797

BONUS FACT: When he personally put down the Whiskey Rebellion in 1791, Washington became the only sitting American president who would ever actively command an army in the field. Luckily, he was able to end the rebellion peacefully, without having to fire a shot.

The Invasion of Canada

America on the Attack

Quebec, Canada
June 1775–October 1776

> Arnold's expedition has been marked with such scenes of misery that it requires a stretch of faith to believe that human nature was equal to them.

—Delegate William Hooper, Second Continental Congress

I N 1775, THE AMERICAN COLONIES TRIED TO conquer Canada and make it the Fourteenth Colony. They almost succeeded.

Nowadays we like to think of Canada as our friendly neighbor to the north. A quiet, peaceful land of lumberjacks, grizzly bears, and professional hockey players who only *occasionally* haul off and start punching each other in the face for no apparent reason. But back in the early days of the American Revolution, the Great White North was still a loyal British colony, and the only way America was going to bring it the glorious liberty of democracy was by sending thousands of guys with guns to march all over Quebec and stab the land into submission with their bayonets.

Fresh off a (sort of) victory over British regular troops in Boston, the Americans were super-stoked about the idea of launching a massive surprise attack north into Canada to capture it. Attacking Canada was probably the last thing the British would ever have expected, and the land was pretty ripe for the taking—the British had somewhere between five hundred and eighteen hundred guys stuck trying to defend an area that is about three times the size of France. Plus, Quebec was largely settled by French Canadians, and the colonists were pretty convinced that those guys were just dying for a chance to help America fight the British. Newly appointed Continental Army commander George Washington decided on a two-pronged attack. One group would go north along Lake Champlain and attack Montreal. The other would have a much more difficult task ahead of it.

Colonel Benedict Arnold was already a superstar celebrity in the Continental Army. Tales of his bravery during the capture of Fort Ticonderoga were the stuff of legend, and he had earned a reputation for being completely fearless. As one of his soldiers put it, this guy was the sort of commander who said "Follow me!" at a time when other leaders were happy saying "Go get 'em, boys!" A successful and super-rich merchant before the war, Arnold was so excited about commanding the attack on Canada that he volunteered to lead one of the most daring expeditions ever undertaken. He was going to take one thousand soldiers on a 350-mile canoe journey through the completely uncharted wilderness and surprise-attack the Canadian capital, Quebec City. It was dangerous, full of impossible hazards, and almost completely suicidal. But if the operation was successful,

Benedict Arnold, engraved by Henry Bryan Hall, Sr., after a painting by John Trumbull

he would catch the British completely off guard, capture their capital, and set the table for Canada to become an American colony.

Benedict Arnold departed present-day Augusta, Maine, on September 25, 1775. He had a thousand soldiers and several hundred tons of food, ammunition, and supplies with him. Everything was loaded into more than two hundred large bateaux (kind of like flat-bottomed canoes) that Arnold had bought with his own money. He personally commanded one group, while the other was led by his lieutenant, a hulking Virginian named Daniel Morgan. Morgan was a mountain of a man who used a lot of bad language, found himself in tavern brawls all the time, and once got in trouble during the French and Indian War for knocking out a higher-ranking officer with one punch. But his soldiers all loved and respected him because he told really funny jokes and could beat up any man who defied him. Also, he kind of looked like a comic-book villain because half of his teeth had been shot out when he took a musket ball to the face in 1758.

The 350-mile journey through the deadly wilderness from Augusta to Quebec City is completely insane to think about. A thousand Colonial soldiers in flat-bottomed rowboats headed down the Kennebec River, making their way past waterfalls and through white-water rapids. Sometimes they had to get out of the boats and drag them around a particularly difficult patch of the river, and other times they risked it and went prow-first into deadly waterways. They were pelted by freezing rain, marched through knee-deep mud, and dragged their boats through Canadian snowstorms. Some of the canoes sank, and others flipped over, ruining the gunpowder or food supplies they were carrying. By the time the troops left the Kennebec and started going up the Dead River, many of them were completely out of food. Men starved to death, froze, got sick, or simply said "Forget this" and turned back for home. They were eating candle wax, soap, and shoe leather to keep themselves alive.

On October 21, after almost a month of this horrific journey, a huge rainstorm flooded what was left of the Colonial supplies. All the men had a big meeting to decide whether they should keep going, but Benedict Arnold gave a super-impressive pump-up speech and urged the Americans to complete their mission. Against all odds, they somehow made it out, arriving at the Canadian town of Sertigan on October 30. Arnold immediately used his own money to buy food for the entire army, which was now only six hundred men.

Now all they had to do was find a way to capture the most secure fortress in North America.

The Americans marched for two more weeks until they got to the Saint Lawrence River; then they built more canoes, snuck across the river and past British warships in the middle of the night, and finally caught their first glimpse of the city.

Covered by snow in the dead of the soul-crushing Canadian winter, Quebec City was a full-scale castle fortress surrounded by a forty-foot stone wall with three gates, six huge towers, and over two hundred cannons. It was defended by eighteen hundred Canadian and British soldiers under the command of Colonel Allan MacLean, a ferocious Scottish Highlander with tons of combat experience.

If you ever want to know what kind of man Benedict Arnold was, here's something to think about. Arnold had six hundred men with him. They were exhausted and freezing. Most of his powder had been ruined, so he had enough for each of his guys to shoot five shots. He didn't have any cannons. One hundred of his muskets had been destroyed in the journey.

He still sent a messenger to the walls of Quebec City to formally demand its unconditional surrender.

Colonel MacLean responded by whizzing a cannonball very close to the messenger's head.

Seeing that he wasn't going to persuade these guys to surrender, Arnold wisely decided to chill out and wait for reinforcements from Brigadier General Richard Montgomery, who had actually captured Montreal a few weeks earlier without much of a fight. Montgomery was a tall, handsome Irish aristocrat (his dad was a baronet!) who had committed himself to the American cause. He had personally led his troops through the swamps, rain-soaked forests, and deadly wilderness surrounding Lake Champlain, then laid siege to the forts surrounding Montreal. The British governor of Canada decided he couldn't waste the manpower trying to defend both Montreal and Quebec City and abandoned Montreal to the Americans. So when Montgomery met up with Benedict Arnold outside Quebec City on December 2, 1775, with boatloads of supplies, weapons, winter clothing, and soldiers, it quickly became clear that the fate of Canada was going to be decided here.

On New Year's Eve 1775, in the middle of a horrible white-out snowstorm, the Americans made a daring attack to storm Quebec City. One small force fired on the main defenses, trying to trick the defenders into thinking they were the big attack, while two large groups of soldiers swung around the sides of the fortress to attack through the town itself. Arnold's group took the north route, and Montgomery's group took the south. The plan was for both American armies to fight through the city streets, meet up in the middle of town, and then attack the main fort together. It was insanely dangerous, and every guy there knew it. The day before the battle, every soldier in the Colonial Army had written the words *Liberty or Death* on a piece of paper and had pinned it to his hat to remind the world of what they were fighting for.

It quickly became obvious to the Americans that capturing Canada was, in fact, not agreeable to the Canadians. Old men, young boys, housewives, and schoolgirls all rushed to

COLONEL BENEDICT ARNOLD

QUEBEC 1775

BRIGADIER GENERAL
RICHARD MONTGOMERY

the defense of Quebec City. They fired muskets from the windows, threw pots and pans from the rooftops, and rushed ammunition to the British defenders as the Americans forced their way through the city streets. In the northern part of the city, Arnold and his men stormed toward a barricade, ripping a hole through it with a cannon that Arnold had mounted on the back of a sled.

Daniel Morgan, meanwhile, threw a ladder up onto the walls of a small fort, screaming for his men to follow. The second he got to the top, a Canadian shot at him at such close range that the fire from the end of the musket burned Morgan's face. He fell off the ladder, got super-mad, climbed back to the top, and immediately started fighting with his sword. With a cheer, his men followed. The swirling blizzard had soaked a lot of the soldiers' gunpowder and rifles, so many Americans were resorting to fists and bayonets to break through the barricade.

Suddenly, as Benedict Arnold stood at the front of his men, screaming for them to push forward, a Canadian musket ball slammed into his leg. As his men pulled their wounded commander back to safety, Arnold shouted for Morgan to take over and continue the attack.

In the south, Richard Montgomery didn't fare any better. His men had also run into a British barricade, but the barricade's last remaining Canadian defender pulled the cord to fire the barricade's cannon. The gun ripped off a blast

of small pellets called grapeshot, and it filled the city street with hundreds of iron chunks about the size of Ping-Pong balls. The blast killed Montgomery, who was at the head of his men, as well as most of his officers. One of Montgomery's assistants—future US vice president Aaron Burr—apparently grabbed the fallen American general and tried to pull his body away but eventually had to give up and abandon him. The next-highest-ranking American officer, Colonel Donald

Campbell, having just seen his commander get epically blown away, ordered his group to retreat.

On the other side of Quebec City, Daniel Morgan had no idea that he was now all alone, fighting through a hostile city with British forces closing in on him from every direction. The hulking Virginian just pressed on, screaming, fighting, capturing cannons, and kicking in doors. As one of his men wrote, "Betwixt every peal the awful voice of Morgan is heard, whose gigantic stature and terrible appearance carries disarray among the foe wherever he comes."

Morgan and his men captured a second barricade, but in the blinding snowstorm he got slightly lost in the maze of city streets. As he fought from house to house, the British eventually surrounded him. With most of his men either dead or captured, Morgan finally found himself backed up against a wall, holding his sword out as nearly a dozen British soldiers demanded his surrender. Morgan, defiant to the end, dared any one of those redcoats to try to take his sword from him. But in the end his men begged him to stand down and give up.

As dawn rose on the year 1776, Benedict Arnold sat in a field hospital outside the walls of Quebec City, listening to victory bells celebrating the American defeat. Arnold's entire detachment had been killed, wounded, or captured. He'd been up all night having surgery to remove a musket ball from his ankle. And of the three thousand Americans who had attacked Canada, only eight hundred remained.

Arnold maintained the siege a few months longer, waiting for reinforcements that would never come. After a few weeks, the snow on the Canadian rivers began to melt, and the British got around the siege by sailing transports into town with more soldiers and supplies. For all his heroic bravery and epic adventuring, Arnold knew that this was a battle he could not win. He ordered his forces to retreat to America. Canada would remain a British colony.

The forty-foot walls of Quebec City were never breached by the Americans. They stand to this very day.

BEEN THERE, DONE THAT

The American attack of 1775 wasn't the first time Quebec had been assaulted by a hostile invasion force. The first Battle of Quebec actually took place sixteen years earlier, as the final battle of the French and Indian War. Led by fearless commander James Wolfe, the British Army scrambled up the Saint Lawrence River and attacked the French garrison at Quebec on September 13, 1759. In a long, grueling battle that killed both Wolfe and the commander of the French garrison, the British overran the enemy and took Quebec, breaking the power of France in the New World and sealing the French and Indian War for England.

Not As Simple As You'd Think

America tried to conquer Canada again during the War of 1812. But not only did the Canadians and the British turn back an American invasion force, they also captured Detroit from the Americans *and* burned Washington, DC, to the ground—including the White House and the Capitol (which housed the Library of Congress). Think about that the next time you want to make fun of Canadians for being too polite.

Cannon Fever

Running full-speed straight toward a gigantic iron cannon while it's ripping off high explosives and steel shrapnel at you is probably one of the most terrifying things a person can do. A lot of soldiers in the war got really messed up in the head by this sort of thing. After surviving a couple of battles, it was common for some men to get so scared by the idea of fighting again that they would have to go lie down in the army field hospital for a while. During World War I this condition was called "shell shock," but in the Revolutionary War it was called "cannon fever." Today we call it PTSD (post-traumatic stress disorder).

The Battle of Lake Champlain

My whole thoughts are now bent on making a safe retreat out of this country; however, I hope we shall not be obliged to leave it until we have had one bout more for the honour of America.

**—Brigadier General Benedict Arnold,
Continental Army, May 31, 1776**

After the defeat at Quebec City, Benedict Arnold couldn't just chill and wait for his gunshot wound to heal. He was now the main guy in charge, he'd lost half his army, and as soon as the Canadian ice started to melt, he knew he was going to be attacked by a huge group of British reinforcements arriving from England. He had to get his men the heck out of there quickly, and he had to do everything he could to delay the enemy.

So Arnold skillfully headed back south toward America, burning bridges and destroying supplies along the way to slow the British advance. His actions delayed a British attack for months, and it wasn't until October 1776 that Arnold heard news that the British were sailing thirteen thousand men on twenty-nine warships down Lake Champlain.

He was at the end of his rope, out of time and supplies,

but Arnold had to do something. The only problem was that he didn't have any ships, didn't have any sailors, and didn't have any of the things you'd need to build ships. Like wood, nails, and sails. Makes it kind of tough, you know?

No problem. He put out a call for help to all the people around him, had his soldiers chop down trees, melted down horseshoes and gun barrels to make nails, and somehow miraculously managed to place sixteen warships on Lake Champlain. He grabbed a group of New Hampshire infantry soldiers, taught them how to sail, and then attacked the British Invasion Fleet on October 11, 1776.

Fighting an epic, seven-hour battle against the British, Benedict Arnold's forces did everything they could with their makeshift warships. Their boats were smashed, blown up, and set on fire left and right, but still the ragtag band of American sailors fought back, retreated, fought again, retreated more.

Benedict Arnold lost every single ship in his fleet. Some of them he destroyed himself so the British wouldn't capture them. Most of them were blown up. He carried his wounded men home to America wrapped in the bloody sails of the ships, but his daring attack had been a complete success. He settled down to defend Fort Ticonderoga, knowing that his actions had delayed the British advance by two weeks. Now it was again too cold and icy for them to keep coming. The British had to make camp for the winter and didn't attempt to invade south into America until the spring of 1777.

And when they did, the Americans were ready for them.

Know Your Founding Fathers

NAME: John Adams

BIRTHDAY: October 30, 1735

BIRTHPLACE: Braintree, Massachusetts

CLAIM TO FAME: Second president of the United States

JOB BEFORE THE WAR: Lawyer and politician

ROLE IN THE WAR: Leading member of the Second Continental Congress

AFTER THE WAR: Vice president to George Washington; president of the United States from 1797 to 1801

BONUS FACT: He originally suggested that the official title of the president should be "His Highness, the President of the United States, and Protector of the Rights of the Same." Nobody else really thought this was a good idea.

A Declaration of Independence

America Proclaims Its Freedom

Philadelphia, Pennsylvania
June 11–July 4, 1776

> Yesterday the greatest question was decided which ever was debated in America; and a greater perhaps never was, nor will be, decided among men. A resolution was passed without one dissenting colony, "that these United Colonies are, and of right ought to be, free and independent States."
>
> —Delegate John Adams, Second Continental Congress

BACKING UP A BIT, A FEW MONTHS BEFORE Benedict Arnold ended up at Fort Ticonderoga, in the searing-hot, un-air-conditioned Pennsylvania State House, the Second Continental Congress was assembled, desperately trying to figure out what the goat cheese they were going to do next.

As the semiofficial government of the rebellion, the Continental Congress had already made some pretty key decisions. They'd ordered the attack on Canada, which had come really close to succeeding. They'd appointed George Washington to lead the army. And with news of the capture of Boston for the rebellion, the three hundred men of the Congress were feeling pretty good about themselves. But everything was happening very fast, and with reports that King George was coming for them, the Congress needed to figure out how they were going to continue with this war.

In early June 1776, one man stood at the front of the Congress and gave a super-mega pump-up speech about something that had only been hinted at before: American independence. Passionately arguing his case, John Adams (remember his earlier speech about how the colonies should unite against England?) said that this was the point of the entire thing: to free America from the shackles of a tyrannical dictator and to create our own country based on the principles of democracy.

Democracy is the form of government where people in a country get to vote for the leadership of the country. It's the style we have now, with a president, Congress (made up of the Senate and the House of Representatives), state governors, state legislatures, etc., all of whom get voted for by the people. While it might seem pretty normal to you and me sitting here in the twenty-first century, in 1776 there were zero countries in the world that did this. *Everyone* had a king. Sure, Britain had a Parliament that voted on things, but at the end of the day these weren't completely free societies—every country from France to England to even China had a single person who called the shots. To many of the people in America, the idea of democracy was one step away from total chaos.

There were tons of questions. What would democracy look like? Didn't the colonies need England to survive? Would the people even support democracy? How would they start the process of setting up a system of government that nobody had ever seen before? And what would stop some guy from just declaring himself king and taking over?

There were a lot of folks who argued against Adams. They said, "No, dude, slow your roll, let's not get all crazy here. We won Bunker Hill, we captured Boston, and now King George is going to send his army over here to kick our butts, burn our cities to the ground, then hang everyone as traitors. This is the perfect time to talk peace. Stop this brutal fighting and figure out some deal where we stay part of the British Empire and still get all the things we decided to fight over in the first place."

John Adams didn't want to hear that, and by June 1776 many of the people in America didn't, either. The best-selling reading material at this time in the colonies was a forty-seven-page pamphlet written by an Englishman named

Thomas Paine. It was called *Common Sense*, and this thing was like an ultimate rap battle about why kings suck and people should get rid of them. Paine was a British reporter who had left school when he was twelve years old, and Americans loved his pamphlet because it was short, it was exciting, and it didn't use a bunch of fancy language to try to sound smart. Also, it was cool to have a copy because the British were allowed to arrest you for having it, and people love it when they can get away with doing something they're not supposed to. By the time John Adams gave his speech to the Continental Congress, there were over seventy-five thousand copies of this booklet floating around, and a decent chunk of Americans were super-into the idea of ditching the king and ruling over themselves for a change.

The debates went back and forth for weeks, but finally, on June 11, 1776, the Continental Congress decided to vote on the most critical decision of the entire American Revolution: whether or not the colonies would declare their independence from Great Britain.

The men of the Continental Congress all knew that if they voted for independence and America lost the war, every man in the room could be executed for treason. As delegate Benjamin Franklin joked, "We must hang together, or most assuredly we shall all hang separately."

Every single member voted in support of American independence. They were going to totally go for it. They were

going to be free, independent from Great Britain forever. No longer would they be "the British Colonies of America." They would be "the United States of America."

Now all that was left was to put it in writing.

The Continental Congress selected five men to actually put together the letter that would proclaim American independence. In the small second-floor living room of an ordinary-looking brick building in Philadelphia, the group assembled: lawyer John Adams of Massachusetts, famous Pennsylvania writer and inventor Benjamin Franklin, a Connecticut businessman named Roger Sherman, a New York judge named Robert Livingston, and a Virginia lawyer named Thomas Jefferson.

After a few hours of discussion, the group chose Thomas Jefferson to write one of the most important documents in American history.

Thomas Jefferson was like, "No way." He and Adams got into an argument, with each guy trying to persuade the other dude to write it. Finally, after a quick debate, Adams gave his reasons why it should be Jefferson: "Reason first, you are a Virginian, and a Virginian ought to appear at the head of this business. Reason second, I am obnoxious, suspected, and unpopular. You are very much otherwise. Reason third, you can write ten times better than I can."

Jefferson didn't argue. Instead, he got to work.

Thirty-three-year-old Thomas Jefferson was highly

intelligent and came from a wealthy Virginian family, but he was really not a good public speaker or debater. What he could do, however, was write crazy well. He'd had a few articles published, and most of them were incredibly well-done essays about why Americans should be free. But surrounded by ultra-famous lawyer John Adams and a superstar author like Benjamin Franklin, you can imagine he would have been kind of nervous. I mean, imagine that these guys are trying to say that *you're* the guy to single-handedly write a letter to the king of England telling him to pound sand. It's the ultimate breakup letter on behalf of a few million people, and a lot of them are going to be killed because of it. I'd be pretty freaked out, too.

Thomas Jefferson gritted his teeth, grabbed his feather quill, dipped it in some black ink, and went to work. For the next few days, he scribbled, scratched, corrected, paced the room, and asked his buddies for advice on difficult phrasings.

When it was read in front of the Continental Congress in early July 1776, everyone got goose bumps.

If you ever decide to visit the National Archives in Washington, DC (and you totally should if you get the chance), you can see the actual Declaration of Independence in person. It's in an airtight, bulletproof case, on display with the Constitution and the Bill of Rights. You'll probably be surprised when you see it, because it's really not that big. It's one page long. But the moment it was accepted by the

Continental Congress—on July 4, 1776—is the moment the United States of America was officially created. Here's what it said:

> When in the Course of human events it becomes
> necessary for one people to dissolve the political
> bands which have connected them with another
> and to assume among the powers of the earth,
> the separate and equal station to which the
> Laws of Nature and of Nature's God entitle
> them, a decent respect to the opinions of
> mankind requires that they should declare the
> causes which impel them to the separation. We

*hold these truths to be self-evident, that all
men are created equal; that they are endowed
by their Creator with inherent and inalienable
Rights; that among these, are Life, Liberty,
and the pursuit of Happiness.*

It then goes on to lay out all the bad stuff King George did to the colonies, why his actions are illegal under British law, and why the American colonies are completely justified in overthrowing him. It says that the Americans did everything they could to try to talk things out peacefully, but then finishes with this:

*We, therefore, the Representatives of the united
States of America, in General Congress,
Assembled, appealing to the Supreme Judge of
the world for the rectitude of our intentions, do,
in the Name, and by Authority of the good
People of these Colonies, solemnly publish and
declare, That these United Colonies are, and of
Right ought to be Free and Independent States;
that they are Absolved from all Allegiance
to the British Crown, and that all political
connection between them and the State of Great
Britain, is and ought to be totally dissolved;
and that as Free and Independent States,*

*they have full Power to levy War, conclude
Peace, contract Alliances, establish Commerce,
and to do all other Acts and Things which
Independent States may of right do. And for
the support of this Declaration, with a firm
reliance on the protection of divine Providence,
we mutually pledge to each other our Lives, our
Fortunes and our sacred Honor.*

The document was accepted by Congress with just thirty-nine changes to Jefferson's original draft, the most significant one being that the Congress took out a part about abolishing slavery in the colonies, and they also took out a part about how all Americans should hate all British people forever. The final Declaration eventually received fifty-six signatures from all thirteen colonies, each man knowing that adding his name to the document meant certain death if the Revolution failed. The largest of all the signatures was that of our friend John Hancock from Boston—he signed it super-huge, threw down his quill, and joked, "There! King George should be able to read that without glasses!"

Copies of the Declaration of Independence were immediately run off from printing presses across Philadelphia, stuffed into horses' saddlebags, and rushed all throughout the colonies. When it was read at the Boston State House, the colonists cheered and fired off the cannons at the fort.

Citizens pulled the King's Seal off every government building in the city. When it was read to George Washington's troops camped out in New York City, the soldiers were so pumped they pulled down a bronze statue of King George III and had blacksmiths melt it to make bullets (to shoot at British soldiers). Nowadays we celebrate every July Fourth with hot dogs on the grill, fireworks, and baseball games. But it all goes back to a unanimous vote on a hot, sweaty day in Philadelphia when Thomas Jefferson's document officially created the United States of America.

The Declaration of Independence

Of course, for all the hardships, debating, and arguing, writing the Declaration of Independence was the easy part. The hard part was going to be defending that independence to the death against a very powerful, very angry king who didn't like the idea of ungrateful upstart jerks pulling down his statues and telling him to get lost.

The Noble Turkey

There's a funny story out there claiming that Benjamin Franklin wanted to make the national bird the turkey instead of the bald eagle. This is pretty hilarious if you try to picture what the national seal (called the Great Seal of the United States) on the back of our money would have looked like. But the story isn't exactly true. Franklin didn't like the choice of the eagle, but it was because he thought a bald eagle had "bad moral character" (which is awesome). Bald eagles scavenge the kills of other animals and sometimes get chased off by smaller birds, and even a "silly" bird like the turkey would aggressively defend its turf against a redcoat, according to Franklin. Maybe that's true, but you gotta admit that Thanksgiving would be really weird if we were eating bald eagles instead of turkeys every year.

PROCLAIM LIBERTY THROUGHOUT THE LAND

The Pennsylvania State House is known today as Independence Hall, and it's a really cool museum you should totally check out. During the Revolution, the large bell at the top of the State House tower that called everyone to meetings became known as the Liberty Bell. It's one of the most iconic symbols of American freedom and is inscribed with a passage from the bible: PROCLAIM LIBERTY THROUGHOUT ALL THE LAND UNTO ALL THE INHABITANTS THEREOF (Leviticus 25:10). The bell hung in the steeple of Independence Hall from 1751 to 1846, until a big crack made it unplayable. Now you can visit it in the museum and see the crack, but no person alive today has ever heard the sound the Liberty Bell makes when it rings.

DIPLOMATS AND WARRIORS

Of the 343 members of the Continental Congress, 142 served in the Continental Army as well. One was killed, twelve were wounded, twenty-three were taken prisoner, and two delegates actually switched sides and joined the loyalists.

ALL MEN ARE CREATED EQUAL?

Many of the signers of the Declaration of Independence weren't exactly ready for a completely free society. The freedoms of the Declaration didn't extend to slaves, women, Catholics, or American Indians, for instance, so really it was more of an "all white, Protestant men are created equal" kind of situation. But there were many delegates who fought to free the slaves as part of the Declaration. Thomas Jefferson was one of the most vocal opponents of slavery, even though his family owned them. (Get this: In Virginia in 1775, if you inherited slaves from your parents, by law you literally *could not* set them free even if you wanted to!) John Adams also spoke out about it ferociously. But the sad truth is that there were many plantation owners, particularly in the South, who felt they could not run their farms without slave labor, and they demanded that slavery stick around. Eventually, everyone decided to just leave it out of the Declaration and deal with the slavery subject at a later date (check out *Guts & Glory: The American Civil War* to learn a lot more about this!).

Know Your Founding Fathers

NAME: Thomas Jefferson

BIRTHDAY: April 13, 1743

BIRTHPLACE: Shadwell, Virginia

CLAIM TO FAME: Wrote the Declaration of Independence

JOB BEFORE THE WAR: Lawyer, politician

ROLE IN THE WAR: Served in the Second Continental Congress

AFTER THE WAR: Governor of Virginia from 1779 to 1781;
US secretary of state from 1790 to 1793; vice president of
the United States from 1797 to 1801; and president of the
United States from 1801 to 1809

BONUS FACT: Jefferson doubled the size of the United States
in 1803, when he bought 827,000 square miles of land from
cash-strapped French emperor Napoleon Bonaparte for just
$15 million. This land, known as the Louisiana Purchase,
would make up large portions of the states of Montana,
North Dakota, South Dakota, Minnesota, Wyoming,
Nebraska, Iowa, Missouri, Kansas, Colorado, Oklahoma,
Arkansas, and Louisiana.

The Empire Strikes Back

The Imperials Take Manhattan
Brooklyn, New York
August 26–27, 1776

> Everything breathes the appearance of war. The number of transports are incredible. I believe there are more than 500 of different kinds besides the King's ships—a Force so formidable would make the first power in Europe tremble.
>
> —Vice Admiral Sir George Collier, British Royal Navy

THE **AMERICANS** LOOKED OUT AT THE ENDless armada of towering wooden ships in New York Harbor and realized they were in pretty big trouble. From horizon to horizon, the bay seemed to be completely covered with sails, rigging, cannons, and red-coated soldiers.

Nobody in North America had ever seen a fleet so massive. Over four hundred transport ships of all shapes and sizes had swarmed in from across the Atlantic Ocean, ferrying tens of thousands of rebellion-crushing British soldiers. Small gunboats, frigates, and at least thirty gigantic warships loomed high above the transports, their gunports bristling with never-ending rows of cannons. Open-topped rowboats carried frontline infantry: kilted Scotsmen wearing tall black bearskin hats and blasting patriotic songs on the bagpipes; battle-hardened German mercenaries (soldiers for hire) in pointy brass helmets and blue coats, standing motionlessly at attention; standard English troops in the uniforms of well-known regiments, their brass buttons and leather boots so polished they almost glinted in the sun.

The army was so massive that it took them eight hours to carry twenty-five thousand men into position for their attack.

The American colonies had wanted a fight against the British Empire, and now they were going to get it.

In downtown Manhattan, the heart of New York City, General George Washington watched anxiously as the British were brought across the waterway from Staten Island to Long Island. He had known the attack would come to him, but he'd had no idea how huge it would be. Washington had about twenty thousand troops, all packed so tightly in the streets of New York that there was barely room for horse carts or foot traffic. The patriot sympathizers in town had

been so happy when he arrived that they'd thrown all the loyalist civilians out of their homes. But a few had stayed behind and were now passing notes to the British telling them about what Washington was doing in the city.

Washington had pleaded with Congress for more soldiers to help hold New York City, but there were no men to send him. Now he had to make a stand against an army that outnumbered him and had complete domination of the sea, thanks to its invincible navy. As he deployed his troops evenly between Manhattan Island and Long Island, Washington received a letter from British general William Howe—his old enemy from Boston. Howe told him he could surrender now, and all the patriot fighters would receive a full pardon for their actions and be allowed to go home in peace.

Washington wrote back, "Those who have committed no fault want no pardon."

Okay, fine. Have it your way.

New York City is separated by a set of large rivers. The British landed at Staten Island and set that up as their base of operations. But British commander William Howe had learned his lesson in Boston: Don't give up the high ground. So, instead of attacking Manhattan, he knew he needed to take a place called Brooklyn Heights on Long Island. Washington knew this, too, and positioned his best troops there to fight off the assault.

Except he failed to defend one of the passes that led up to Brooklyn Heights.

General Howe lined up most of his guys like they were going to run straight up the hill at the Americans (just like they did at Bunker Hill), but then he sent General Henry Clinton around to look for a secret way behind the enemy forces. Clinton's cavalry scouts found four passes leading up to Brooklyn Heights, and one was guarded by just five American horsemen. Washington didn't have enough guys to cover every pass effectively, so he'd put these guys there with orders to take off and warn the rest of the army at the first sight of the enemy.

They never made it. The five American riders were attacked by British cavalrymen. The Americans bolted, but they weren't fast enough. All five riders were captured before they could spread the word. That night, under the cover of complete darkness, General Henry Clinton marched ten thousand men and twenty-six cannons through the pass.

As dawn broke on the morning of August 27, 1776, American general John Sullivan awoke to find half the British Army lined up in full battle array behind him. At the same moment, the Scottish and German mercenaries at the bottom of the heights began their attack from the front.

The Americans didn't have a chance, but they fought like demons anyway. Shooting in both directions, Sullivan's warriors battled the charging Germans while the British artillery blasted through them from the flanks and the rear. Clinton's cannons ripped out blasts of grapeshot into American lines.

From the front, the German forces of General Leopold Philip von Heister lowered their bayonets in perfect order, charging forward with a bloodcurdling scream. Sullivan's men had no bayonets, but they pulled knives and swung their rifles. Sullivan hurled himself into the fray, firing a pistol in each hand, but he was captured, and von Heister's stone-cold German mercenaries cut their way through the patriots. In some cases, they even bayonetted men who were trying to surrender.

Soon the entire American line was running for its life. Things were looking really bad, with many men dead, wounded, captured, or fleeing in terror. In this madness, one man rose up to save the Continental Army—a man known to history simply as Lord Stirling.

Lord Stirling's real name was William Alexander, but I guess on a trip to England in 1756 he came across research that led him to believe he was the senior male descendant of the First Earl of Stirling, so in the 1760s he started referring to himself as Lord Stirling. This really ticked off the British House of Lords, who thought he was full of crap and refused to recognize his claim. And now, ironically, Lord Stirling was holed up in a stone house on the edge of Brooklyn Heights fighting against the Scottish soldiers of the Forty-Second Black Watch—one of the most dangerous and elite regiments in the history of the British Army.

Lord Stirling, along with four hundred men from Delaware

**A modern reconstruction of the Vechte-Cortelyou House, known
as the Old Stone House, located in Brooklyn, New York**

and Maryland, had thrown up a quick line of defense to cover
the American retreat. Shooting through the windows of the
house, firing from behind rocks, trees, and an old fence, the
small group loaded and fired as fast as it could. The Black
Watch came on with charge after charge, but every advance
was cut down with crippling gunfire. Against all odds, the
Americans held, fighting off the enemy and preventing a massacre of the entire American army.

Then von Heister's Germans arrived and charged forward alongside the Watch. George Washington was receiving reports from his base on Manhattan Island and simply said, "Good God, what brave fellows I must this day lose."

After holding out for hours, Lord Stirling and his men could not withstand the full might of the British forces. Surrounded by enemies, the stone house on fire, and most of his force dead or dying, Lord Stirling surrendered his sword to General von Heister personally. Only a few of his Marylanders escaped,

and only by swimming across the river to Manhattan Island. The Battle of Brooklyn had cost twelve hundred American casualties to just four hundred British. But it might have been much, much worse without Lord Stirling.

As night fell, General Howe sent another letter to Washington demanding surrender. Washington wouldn't hear it. In one of the great engineering efforts of all military history, Washington had the "Marvelous Men from Marblehead"—a regiment of former New England sailors and whalers—ferry nine thousand troops across the East River in just twelve hours. Through darkness, gun smoke, and fog, the New Englanders rowed dozens of trips back and forth, sneaking the remains of the Continental Army out of Howe's trap right under the nose of the British Navy. When the sun rose and Howe saw Washington's army safely on Manhattan Island, he couldn't believe it.

But the damage had been done. General Howe had won a crushing victory over the Americans, taking New York City (and eventually parts of New York State and New Jersey) for England. Washington had been out-generaled and had seen his army smashed. A lot of demoralized patriots went home. Others had fought to the death or been captured. Many of Washington's best generals were now prisoners.

He had gone into the campaign with twenty thousand soldiers. Between battle deaths, captured soldiers, and desertion, when he went into winter quarters (in this period, armies didn't really fight in the winter) in November 1776, his army was less than three thousand strong.

> The time is now near at hand which must
> probably determine whether Americans are to
> be free men or slaves; whether they are to have
> any property they can call their own; whether
> their homes and farms are to be pillaged and
> destroyed and themselves consigned to a state
> of wretchedness from which no human efforts
> can deliver them. The fate of unborn millions
> will now depend, under God, on the conduct
> and courage of this army....We have therefore to
> resolve to conquer or die.
>
> —George Washington, July 2, 1776

BE CAREFUL WHAT YOU WISH FOR

After the British took over New York City, many loyalists in the city were relieved that they were once again under the protection of the king's troops. But that went out the door pretty quickly, because the British and Hessians (another name for the German mercenaries) started taking over buildings and houses like they owned the place, looting expensive stuff from structures that had been abandoned. Even worse, instead of thanking loyalists for their help as spies and informants, the British treated the loyalists with suspicion, arresting some of them and accusing them of being patriots in disguise. Many people who had supported the king quickly changed their tune and started working as spies for the rebellion.

HIRED MUSCLE

Even though there were a huge number of German soldiers in the British Army, Germany wasn't officially ever at war with the colonies. In fact, Germany wasn't even a country—it was a mishmash of a bunch of smaller states, each run by its own prince (go back to the introduction for more about this). King George needed more guys, so he made a deal with several German princes to borrow soldiers for the war. These mercenaries mostly came from the German state of Hesse-Kassel, which is why we call them Hessians. They honestly didn't care about the outcome of the war—they just wanted to make money—so they became known for plundering, looting, and stabbing prisoners. You can probably guess that this ticked off a lot of Americans. But later in the war, the American government offered Hessian troops land and money to abandon the British, and many of them bailed, took their farms, and spent the rest of their lives living in the land of the free.

PICK YOUR POISON

Cannons at this time could fire a number of different types of ammunition. *Solid shot* was a regular cannonball like you see in cartoons. A crazy thing about solid shot, though, is that it bounces like a basketball when it hits the ground! So artillerymen would aim low and try to bounce the cannonball to cut people's legs out from under them. *Grapeshot* was a packet of hundreds of grape-sized iron balls that scattered in every direction when they came out of the barrel. The range on this type of ammunition wasn't great, but it turned the cannon into a big, terrifying shotgun that basically tore apart anything within two hundred yards of the barrel. *Shells* were hollow cannonballs filled with explosives and a fuse that blew up like a hand grenade when they hit something. *Red-hot shot* was typically used on navy ships. Guys would put a cannonball in an oven until it got so hot it started glowing red; then they used tongs (like the ones for your BBQ) to load it into the cannon. When the burning-hot mass of horrible destruction hit a wooden ship, the heat of the cannonball would set the ship on fire almost immediately.

Know Your Founding Fathers

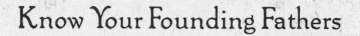

NAME: William Alexander, Sixth Earl of Stirling

BIRTHDAY: 1726

BIRTHPLACE: New York City, New York

CLAIM TO FAME: Commander of the American rear guard at Long Island

JOB BEFORE THE WAR: Owned mining, agriculture, and winemaking businesses

ROLE IN THE WAR: Commanded the First Maryland Regiment, later became a major general

AFTER THE WAR: Did not survive; died of illness on January 15, 1783

BONUS FACT: Even though his title was disputed, Alexander led his life as though he was a member of the Scottish nobility, and every Colonial soldier referred to him simply as Lord Stirling. He did not survive the war, so when his daughter got married she was walked down the aisle by George Washington himself.

8

Crossing the Delaware

The Battle of Trenton
Trenton, New Jersey
December 26, 1776

> Brother Benjamin is off in France.
> We're taking Trenton back again.
> The garrison of Hessians will fall.
> They say Delaware will freeze a man.
>
> —Astronautalis, "Trouble Hunters"

DECEMBER 1776. THE CONTINENTAL ARMY had faced the full might of the British Army, and they'd been demolished. In the freezing cold of the New Jersey winter, the wounded, sick, exhausted Continental Army of George Washington retreated. They were low on ammunition, without wool coats, and "so destitute of shoes that the blood left on the frozen ground, in many places, marked the route they had taken."

The Americans were chased hard every step of the way by the British Army, who pursued the rebels relentlessly both on foot and on horseback. Along the way, the British captured provisions, commandeered buildings, plundered villages, and set up bases and garrisons all throughout New York and New Jersey. Local people soon became worried that they'd get in trouble for helping the rebels, and they stopped offering food, warm blankets, or supplies. American soldiers deserted or accepted the British offer for forgiveness and simply gave up. The army of George Washington, once so pumped up from the Declaration of Independence and a heroic victory at Bunker Hill, was now freezing to death and worried that this was a war it had no chance of winning. Even the Continental Congress was freaked out. It abandoned the suddenly threatened city of Philadelphia and moved the capital of America to Baltimore, Maryland.

Under anyone else, the Continental Army would have completely disintegrated. But George Washington wasn't about to give up the struggle for freedom quite so easily.

As I mentioned earlier, armies in the old days didn't usually fight during the winter. It was too cold for the men, and the snow, rain, and ice made it difficult to move horses, cannons, wagons, and all the other stuff they needed. So on December 14, 1776, the British commander ordered his men to set up camp for the winter. All throughout New York and New Jersey, British forces did just that.

Washington camped out on the south side of the Delaware River for a little over a week. Across the water he could see the British garrison at the city of Trenton, New Jersey. And he decided he was going to do something crazy....

He was going to attack.

On the surface, his plan was insane. He didn't have enough ships. He didn't have enough men. The Hessian troops that were encamped there were better trained, more experienced, and better equipped, and they'd be able to blast the Americans out of the water if they noticed Washington crossing the river.

The entire plan was so over-the-top bonkers that when British general James Grant passed along a rumor that Washington was planning to attack Trenton, Hessian commander Colonel Johann Rall simply laughed and said, "Let them come."

They did.

Around midnight on Christmas night, in a driving wind- and rainstorm, a force of twenty-four hundred American soldiers assembled on the south bank of the Delaware River about sixteen miles north of Trenton. Each man was carrying sixty rounds of ammunition and three days of food. Screaming orders over the wind and rain, Colonel Henry Knox directed the Continentals into large, forty-foot boats, rocking in the current of the powerful Delaware River.

John Glover and the "Marvelous Men from Marblehead" steered the pointed bows of the ships through the freezing cold water, dodging huge chunks of ice. A single false step by any of the Marblehead pilots could have ripped a hole in their boat, sending sixty men into water so cold it would almost certainly kill them right away. Henry Knox had other ships loaded with cannons, horses, cannonballs, and artillery caissons (chests that hold ammunition), and somehow miraculously ferried eighteen full-sized cannons and fifty horses across the river in boats that were in no way designed to carry that sort of thing.

As the men rowed through the biting cold wind, pulling their coats about them for warmth, they saw an image at the head of their formation that would forever be part of American history: Their commander in chief, General George Washington, was standing tall in the prow of the lead ship, willing his men to follow him.

When the sun rose over the town of Trenton, New Jersey, on the morning of December 26, 1776, the German sentries were startled by the appearance of something they could never have expected to see: George Washington, twenty-four

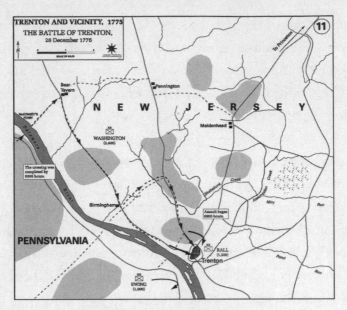

Map of the Battle of Trenton

hundred American soldiers, and eighteen fully manned artillery cannons charging screaming out of the forest to the north of the city, guns blazing and flags waving in the driving snowstorm.

Blitzing from every direction, the Americans hit the city from the north, south, and west all at the same time, pounding it with gunfire. Three regiments of Hessian infantry rolled out of their beds and garrisons, grabbed their rifles, and raced out into the streets, desperately trying to figure out what the heck was going on. One company entered the main street of town just in time to see Henry Knox slamming his

cannons around the corner and opening fire. The shots oblit-
erated a storefront and took out part of a building.

A particularly quick-thinking crew of Hessians managed
to get one of their cannons up and running. They wheeled it
into King Street, lined up a juicy shot on the American flank,
then suddenly heard a scream. Charging down a side street
was the Third Virginia Infantry, commanded by Captain
William Washington (George's cousin) and Lieutenant James
Monroe, who would eventually become the fifth president of
the United States. The Hessians spun the twelve-hundred-
pound cannon and fired a shotgun blast head-on into the
Virginians, wounding both Washington and Monroe. But neither man hit the ground. The Third Virginia took the cannon,
turned it around, and fired a shot at the Hessians as they ran.

Colonel Johann Rall was in bed when the fighting began
and ran out into the street to see destruction everywhere. The
fifty-three-year-old mercenary quickly pulled out his sword
and started shouting for his men to fall back through an apple
orchard. But as soon as he got there, he saw another group of
Americans waiting on the other side. He was surrounded.

So he pointed his sword, ordered his men to fix bayonets,
and charged fearlessly into the American army. Rall led the
attack personally.

Henry Knox was ready for him. "We loaded with canister
shot and let them come nearer. We fired all together again
and such destruction it made, you cannot conceive."

Rall was fatally wounded by the cannonade. The rest of his men surrendered to Washington.

The Battle of Trenton only lasted forty-five minutes. The Hessians had twenty-two dead and ninety wounded. About five hundred men escaped. An additional 918 men surrendered to George Washington—not bad considering that Washington only had twenty-four hundred men. The Americans had five men wounded, including Monroe and William Washington. Only two Americans had died, and both of them had frozen to death on the way to the battle.

The Americans looted the German supplies, capturing food, winter clothes, blankets, six cannons, hundreds of guns, bayonets, swords, tons of ammunition, and over seventy barrels of rum. By nightfall on December 26, they'd carried all of it *back* across the Delaware River.

While the Battle of Trenton wasn't a huge strategic victory, it changed the course of the American Revolution and saved the Continental Army. It now had lots of supplies for the winter, and it'd actually beaten the brutal Germans in a fight. The 918 Hessian prisoners were marched through the streets of Philadelphia to the cheers of the crowd. When newspapers came out with reports of an epic American military success in a historic nighttime attack against impossible odds by General George Washington, people all across the colonies realized that this war wasn't over just yet.

AFRICAN-AMERICAN TROOPS AT TRENTON

One of John Glover's Marblehead men was African-American, and there were several black soldiers scattered throughout the Continental regiments, particularly as riflemen in the Twentieth and Twenty-Sixth Continental Infantry Regiments. According to historical records, at least a dozen black soldiers fought at the Battle of Trenton.

PEACE OUT, CORNWALLIS

Washington crossed the Delaware again on December 30, 1776, and this time the British sent a huge force under General Lord Cornwallis to destroy him. After reaching Trenton, Cornwallis camped out on the far side of a river and prepared to attack Washington in the morning, but when he woke up, Washington's army was gone. Their campfires were still burning, but the entire army had bailed in the middle of the night. Cornwallis was like, "What the heck?" Then he started getting reports that Washington's army had marched eighteen miles up the road to Princeton, New Jersey, attacked it, and taken three hundred more British prisoners. The Trenton and Princeton victories combined to inspire the American rebels into thinking maybe they had a chance of winning this war after all.

Presidents in the War

A bunch of future US presidents (plus a couple of guys you'd probably recognize from their portraits on our money) were involved in the American Revolution. Here's the rundown of their roles:

GEORGE WASHINGTON (1st president) was overall commander of American military forces in the war. If you need me to go into more detail on this guy, you haven't been paying attention to the book so far. Nowadays he's on the one-dollar bill *and* on the quarter.

JOHN ADAMS (2nd) was another big-time player, mostly as a diplomat and politician in the Second Continental Congress. He helped write the Declaration of Independence and was part of a group of guys sent to France to negotiate the treaty at the end of the war.

THOMAS JEFFERSON (3rd) wrote the Declaration of Independence, was governor of Virginia, and established the University of Virginia, and his personal library ended up becoming the basis for the Library of Congress. Nowadays he's on the nickel and the two-dollar bill (although you don't see many of those anymore).

JAMES MADISON (4th) was a representative for Virginia in the Second Continental Congress.

JAMES MONROE (5th) was a lieutenant in the Virginia Militia, was wounded by a Hessian cannon at Trenton, and fought at the Battles of New York, Brandywine, and Monmouth.

JOHN QUINCY ADAMS (6th) was John Adams's son. He was just seven years old when the war started, and he and his mother watched the Battle of Bunker Hill from the back porch of their house in Boston. When he was ten, he joined his father on the mission to France to sign the peace treaty ending the war.

ANDREW JACKSON (7th) joined the army at the age of thirteen. His job was to run information back and forth between commanders as a courier. He was captured by the British in 1781. When the British officer who caught Jackson was like, "Hey, kid, clean my boots for me," Jackson said, "Heck no," and the officer got so mad he cut Jackson in the hand with a sword. Jackson is on the front of the twenty-dollar bill today (although not for long! For details on the fascinating person who is replacing him, check out the sections about Harriet Tubman in *Guts & Glory: The American Civil War*).

ALEXANDER HAMILTON, the guy on the ten-dollar bill, was never a president—he was the first secretary of the Treasury. And he was an important actor in the Revolution. Hamilton was with Washington during Trenton and Princeton, assisted Friedrich von Steuben at Valley Forge (more on this in chapter 11), was good friends with the Marquis de Lafayette (coming up in the next chapter!), and led a bayonet attack against British positions at the Battle of Yorktown (check out chapter 20). After the war, he was a key member of the group that wrote the US Constitution.

BENJAMIN FRANKLIN is on the hundred-dollar bill, although he wasn't a president, either. Franklin was a famous writer and inventor, he helped Jefferson with the Declaration of Independence, and he also helped work on the Constitution. Later in the war, Franklin traveled to France to get the French to help America fight the British (chapter 12). His signature is on the peace treaty that ended the war.

So there you have it! Seven American presidents and the faces on most of our currency. The only pieces of money not mentioned here are the fifty-dollar bill (President Ulysses S. Grant, a military hero of the American Civil War), the dime (President Franklin D. Roosevelt, the US president during World War II), the penny (Abraham Lincoln, president during the American Civil War), the half-dollar coin (President John F. Kennedy, who led the nation in the early 1960s), and the five-dollar bill (Lincoln again). Also, it's worth mentioning that even though there were a ton of Clintons in the war (Henry, George, Thomas, etc.), none of them are related to Bill Clinton, the forty-second president of the United States, or to George Clinton, lead singer of the 1970s funk band Parliament-Funkadelic.

Know Your Founding Fathers

NAME: James Monroe

BIRTHDAY: April 28, 1758

BIRTHPLACE: Monroe Hall, Virginia

CLAIM TO FAME: Fifth president of the United States

JOB BEFORE THE WAR: Plantation owner

ROLE IN THE WAR: Fought with the Third Virginia Regiment at Trenton

AFTER THE WAR: Senator; governor of Virginia; US secretary of war; US secretary of state; and president of the United States from 1817 to 1825

BONUS FACT: In that famous painting of George Washington crossing the Delaware, Monroe is the guy holding the American flag.

The Marquis de Lafayette

A Young Foreign Hero Gets His First Taste of Battle

Brandywine, Pennsylvania
September 11, 1777

> When the government violates the people's rights, insurrection is, for the people and for each portion of the people, the most sacred of the rights and the most indispensable of duties.

—Gilbert du Motier, Marquis de Lafayette

O N JUNE 13, 1777, AN ORDINARY-LOOKING courier ship cut its way through the humid night air toward the port city of Georgetown, South Carolina. Not far from the watchful cannons of Charleston, the docks were patrolled by American soldiers and guards, their eyes alert for anything unusual. When the ship landed, twelve men in ordinary, rough clothing walked calmly down the plank to the dock, asked about transportation, and promptly paid for direct travel to Philadelphia, Pennsylvania. They paid in solid gold coins bearing the image of King Louis XVI of France.

Their leader, disguised as a commoner, was a well-read, optimistic nineteen-year-old French Army officer known not by his given name, but by his important French aristocratic title: the Marquis de Lafayette (*Marquis* is pronounced "mar-*kee*"). By the time his adventures were complete, the marquis would be remembered as one of the most influential men in the American Revolution and a national hero both in the United States and in his native France.

Marie-Joseph Paul Yves Roche Gilbert du Motier (yes, that entire thing is his name) was born on September 6, 1757, to a family of incredibly wealthy French nobles. Lafayette was just a baby when his father was killed in battle with the English during the Seven Years' War. When he was thirteen years old, his mom and grandmother both died as well. While this was totally super-horrible, Lafayette then inherited his family estate and was basically a multimillionaire before he turned fourteen. He used some of his money to buy himself a commission in the French Army, enlisting at age fourteen. By nineteen, he was a captain in the French cavalry and was married to a super-rich French noblewoman, meaning that this guy basically had more money than he ever knew what to do with. Like, he used to go to parties with the king of France and stuff.

**Marie-Joseph Paul Yves Roche Gilbert du Motier,
Marquis de Lafayette, painted by Joseph-Désiré Court**

Despite serving in the army for five years, Lafayette never actually saw any combat. So when he heard stories of the American Revolution, he immediately got jacked up out of his mind. Lafayette was a big-time reader of Enlightenment literature (see the sidebar at the end of this chapter for more on that), and he loved the idea of people being free to pursue liberty and independence. He took command of a company of horsemen and used his own money to buy a ship and sail across the sea so they could offer their services to the Continental Army.

Okay, well, yeah, that's great and all, but it's also kind of a problem. You see, Lafayette was a *marquis*, which is the second-highest nonroyal noble title in France, and the British Army would definitely notice this guy running around America with a bunch of French soldiers. They'd probably be so mad about it that they would declare war on France, which is something France *definitely* did not want in 1777.

The king of France caught word of Lafayette's plans and sent men to arrest him. Even worse, British spies heard about the plan, too, and sent a couple of guys to stop him before he could get to America. So in the dead of night, the marquis and eleven of his closest buddies threw on disguises, rode on horseback from Paris to the coast, escaped an attempt to have him arrested, and spent the next two months crossing the Atlantic Ocean trying to dodge British and French ships alike.

After being super-seasick for the entire trip across the Atlantic and then traveling nine hundred miles across the American countryside, the marquis finally reached Philadelphia in July 1777 (Congress had moved the capital back there in March 1777). Dressed like his men in a gold-embroidered military uniform, pressed and shined up with the cool, stylish touches that you can only afford when you're a multi-bajillionaire, Lafayette asked for a chance to fight for American independence. The marquis had no combat experience and didn't speak a lot of English, but, hey, he was

French, powerful, and rich, and he knew the king, and he said he would work for free. So Congress made him a major general and appointed him to serve on the personal staff of General George Washington. Lafayette was so pleased that he donated $200,000 in cash to the American war effort—a sum that would be about *$4.5 million* in today's money.

The Marquis de Lafayette linked up with the Continental Army, and he and GW were good buds pretty much immediately. When Washington asked what Lafayette thought about the war, the young Frenchman simply said, "I am here to learn, not to teach."

Okay, cool, kid. Stick around.

Washington's situation at this time wasn't great. It was six months after the Battle of Trenton, and now that the snow and ice had melted, the British were back on the move. With a huge army heading south from Canada, British overall commander William Howe decided he would take the fight right to Congress and attack Philadelphia itself. He took fifteen thousand soldiers from New York City, loaded them into 260 ships, sailed down to Maryland, and began marching into the heart of the Revolution.

Washington had only about 10,500 men, but he needed to do something to protect the capital. He set up a defense at Brandywine Creek, which according to Google Maps is exactly thirty miles from Independence Hall (where the Second Continental Congress was meeting). Despite its name, this creek was actually a pretty big river. So Washington talked to the farmers in the area, learned there were about eight places where the British could cross, and then set up the American army in perfect positions to defend all eight crossings. His men dug holes, built wooden walls, and prepared for an epic battle to defend their capital against the full force of William Howe's redcoats.

At nine AM on September 11, 1777, American advance scouts were hanging out in an abandoned tavern on the British side of the river when they heard the unmistakable sound of boots crunching and muskets rattling. Four scouts rushed to the window, peered through the gray morning fog, and saw a regiment of Hessian and British Rangers marching in formation up the road. The scouts fired their rifles once and ran for it, leaving their horses behind.

In the American headquarters, in a nice farmhouse about a mile behind the front line, Washington and Lafayette heard the report from the out-of-breath scouts. The British attack was coming, from pretty much where Washington had expected. The commander in chief ordered all his men to load their rifles and cannons and prepare for battle.

On the far side of the river, through the fog, thousands of British regiments formed up for battle over the course of the next couple of hours. At nearly seven thousand men, the group was slightly smaller than the Continental Army lined up against them. The militia (who weren't technically part of the army and didn't report to anyone but still wanted to help) and Continental Army took a deep breath and sighted down their rifles, waiting for the enemy to start their assault.

Around noon another report came to Washington's head-quarters, this time from a local landowner. Apparently, he had seen a group of British soldiers heading way farther up the river, far to the north of the Americans' position. Washington wasn't sure what to do. Maybe it was a trick? Maybe this guy was lying? The local farmers had assured him there was absolutely no way to cross the Brandywine in that direction. Washington sent a small group of scouts to check it out but told most of his men to hold fast and wait for the attack.

Well, we don't know if the local farmers were idiots or trai-tors (they were most likely loyalist sympathizers), but the fact remains that they were really disastrously wrong. William Howe had tons of excellent loyalist spies in the area, and he had been told about a crossing that George Washington didn't believe existed. And on September 11, 1777, General William

Howe and General Lord Cornwallis marched eight thousand fully armed redcoats on a fourteen-mile journey all the way around behind the American lines…and nobody noticed until it was almost too late.

Howe and the Hessians across the river launched their attacks at the exact same time.

Bullets, cannonballs, explosions, and shrapnel filled the sky with tens of thousands of chunks of hot jagged lead all across the Brandywine. Trees were ripped apart by cannon fire, showering leaves, splinters, and branches to the ground. Towering spires of dirt and grass flew high into the air. Men screamed, fired, fought, and died, ripping off shots through white clouds of powder smoke.

The Americans fought heroically, but no army can win when it's being attacked from two directions at the same time. Taking heavy casualties, Washington personally went forward to try to rally his men against Cornwallis and Howe.

Into this fray leapt the young Marquis de Lafayette. Completely ignoring any dangers around him, Lafayette rode his horse hard toward the battle, sweeping past American soldiers who were running for their lives. He reached the front, hopped from his horse, drew his sword, and rallied the troops, ordering them into place and trying to coordinate a more organized withdrawal. He personally led a heroic counterattack, but he didn't have enough men, and the charge was thrown back by Howe's redcoats. During the fighting,

Lafayette took a bullet in the leg, but he refused to leave until he had helped the rest of the embattled division retreat.

Then, suddenly, another foreign hero appeared: a thirty-three-year-old cavalry officer named Casimir Pulaski (remember him from the introduction?). He was a count from Poland who had been a regimental commander during a Polish revolution against Russia in 1768. In that war, he was shot in the arm and slashed in the hand with a sword, escaped arrest in both Turkey and Russia, and came really close to successfully breaking the king of Poland out of a Russian prison. Pulaski's revolution had been crushed, he'd lost his land and his title, and he'd come to America in 1777 to help out. He became the commander of George Washington's thirty-man cavalry bodyguard, and now, with Lafayette and Washington himself in danger, Pulaski came thundering into battle on horseback with a sword in one hand and a pistol in the other. Screaming for Washington and Lafayette to get out, Pulaski and his men jumped over some fences on their horses and crashed into the nearest group of redcoats. Washington later said he believed that this attack by Pulaski saved his life.

The Battle of Brandywine was a terrible defeat for the Continental Army, but it could have been far worse. Heroic actions by Lafayette, Pulaski, and American generals like John Sullivan, "Mad" Anthony Wayne, and Nathanael Greene saved the army from complete destruction. All told, Washington lost about 10 percent of his force. Worse,

however, was that he could no longer defend Philadelphia. The Continental Congress fled to Lancaster, Pennsylvania, and William Howe marched the British into the rebel capital, where he would spend the winter of 1777.

The Marquis de Lafayette had shown incredible bravery in his first taste of combat. George Washington came to visit the young Frenchman in the hospital after the fight and told the surgeon to "treat him as if he were my son." Washington would later promote Lafayette to a field command in the Continental Army, and, as we will see, the marquis played a critical role throughout the rest of the war.

For now, however, the aftermath of Brandywine was kind of like the last scene of *The Empire Strikes Back*: The rebels have taken a nasty defeat, and suffered for it, but they aren't out of this fight just yet.

THE ENLIGHTENMENT

The American Revolution got a lot of its ideas from the French Enlightenment, an intellectual movement in the eighteenth century. It tried to take Europe out of the old-school Middle Ages of kings and move forward into something a little more modern. Led by writers and philosophers like Voltaire, Jean-Jacques Rousseau, Immanuel Kant, Denis Diderot, and Mary Wollstonecraft, the Enlightenment was all about individual liberty, religious tolerance, and focusing on stuff like philosophy, science, reason, and logic, rather than just blindly obeying the strict rules of kings and the Catholic Church. Many of the American Founding Fathers worked hard to apply these ideas to the creation of the United States as a free, enlightened, independent country.

THE CHEW HOUSE

After the defeat at Brandywine, George Washington immediately began planning a counterattack, just like he'd done at Trenton after losing New York. About a month after the fight, Washington sent a huge group of men to attack the British garrison at Germantown, Pennsylvania, but this time it didn't work out so hot for him. One of the lead British units, a group of 120 men from the Fortieth Regiment of Foot, holed themselves up in a two-story stone mansion called the Chew House and simply refused to give up. Led by their commander, Colonel Thomas Musgrave, the Fortieth Regiment fought heroically against thousands of American soldiers, single-handedly stopping Washington's attack and causing confusion everywhere. At one point two groups of American soldiers actually started shooting at each other by mistake! The attack on Germantown was a complete failure, and Washington was forced to fall back once again.

MOVING THE CAPITAL

During the war, the twisting tides of battle forced the Continental Congress to move the American capital a bunch of times:

Philadelphia, Pennsylvania: May 10, 1775–December 12, 1776

Baltimore, Maryland: December 20, 1776–February 27, 1777

Philadelphia, Pennsylvania: March 4, 1777–September 18, 1777

Lancaster, Pennsylvania: September 27, 1777 (one day)

York, Pennsylvania: September 30, 1777–June 27, 1778

Philadelphia, Pennsylvania: July 2, 1778–June 21, 1783

Princeton, New Jersey: June 30, 1783–the end of the war

Know Your Founding Fathers

NAME: Marie-Joseph Paul Yves Roche Gilbert du Motier, Marquis de Lafayette

BIRTHDAY: September 6, 1757

BIRTHPLACE: Chavaniac, France

CLAIM TO FAME: French nobleman who helped win American independence

JOB BEFORE THE WAR: French cavalry officer and wealthy aristocrat

ROLE IN THE WAR: Major general commanding large groups of American troops

AFTER THE WAR: Returned home to France to help enact the French Revolution

BONUS FACT: Lafayette named his only son Georges Washington de Lafayette. The marquis is buried in a famous cemetery in Paris, and the dirt used to cover his coffin was taken from Bunker Hill, Massachusetts.

10

Saratoga

The Turning Point
Saratoga, New York
September 19–October 16, 1777

> The onset of bayonets in the hands of the valiant is irresistible.
>
> —Major General Johnny Burgoyne, British Army

I F YOU WERE A SUPER-RICH BRITISH ARISTO- crat in the eighteenth century and you could pick just one person in the world to invite to your birthday party, you would want it to be British major general Johnny Burgoyne. This guy was tall, handsome, super-cool, confident, and well dressed, and he threw the most amazingly awesome parties in the history of North America. Every guy he met thought he was rad, all the women swooned for him, and pretty much any-time he traveled he took along two horse-drawn wagons full of super-expensive food and drinks and flashy silver dishware. He even had a cool nickname: Gentleman Johnny.

So when this ultimate party monster traveled to London in 1776, hung out at fancy nightclubs all night long with the British minister of war, and then coolly presented his plan to single-handedly win the war against the Americans, you can kind of understand why the minister was like, "Yeah, sounds great to me, dude."

The adventure that resulted would turn into not just the single most important military campaign in the American Revolution, but one of the most important military campaigns in the entire history of the United States of America.

After a few months of preparation, in June 1777, Gentleman Johnny assembled one of the most impressive invasion armies that North America had ever seen. Over seven thousand hardened British, Hessian, Canadian, and American Indian troops all gathered at a base in Canada and prepared for a full-on assault into America. They had 138 cannons (an insanely huge number of guns for that day). Their supply wagons stretched for miles, packed to their ceilings with food, fresh water, wine, rum, silverware, artillery, cannonballs, muskets, writing utensils, paper, and ten thousand other things you might or might not have needed to maintain an army.

The plan was simple: Head south, capture Fort Ticonderoga, smash all rebel resistance up and down the Hudson River Valley, and end up in New York City to celebrate the destruction of the American rebellion with cocktails and those

little shrimps on ice you always see at fancy parties. If necessary, a second force from New York could march north and
squish the rebels between two British armies, but Burgoyne
hardly thought that would be necessary. The plan was so simple that you can almost see the sun glinting off Burgoyne's
perfect teeth as he recited it.

At first, the plan worked great. The American defenders of
Fort Ticonderoga took one look at Burgoyne's insanely huge
number of redcoats and cannons and wagons and horses, and
they basically dropped their guns and ran for it.

But as the British headed farther south, instead of
nice paved roads for his wagons, Burgoyne got backwoods
dirt paths through thick, bug-infested woods and muddy
swampland—not a great situation when you're trying to
drag 138 cannons, dozens of wagons, and almost eight thousand men with any kind of speed. Even worse, the American
commander in northern New York, Philip Schuyler, ordered
his retreating men to make life really hard for the British
by basically doing whatever they could to slow them down.
Every step of the way, Burgoyne ran into destroyed bridges,
burned crops, and logs blocking the road. When his men went
to clear the path, they would get shot at by minutemen hiding in the woods. Even worse, the Americans were sending
raiding parties around behind Burgoyne, trying to cut off the
roads he was using to bring more supplies up to the front.

Another thing working against Johnny was that people

in upstate New York weren't always so happy to see him. Burgoyne put out a call for American Indians and American loyalists to come be part of his army. Well, most Americans in upstate New York had been fighting brutal warfare *against* the American Indians for, like, a hundred years. Since Burgoyne wanted the American Indians with him, the former loyalists decided to join up with the rebels instead. Still, this overconfident pretty boy had never failed at anything in his life and wasn't about to start now. Even as American minutemen started to move around behind him, he issued a written order to his troops. It simply said *This Army Will Not Retreat.*

Stubbornly pushing forward, Burgoyne eventually ran into the Continental Army at a place called Bemis Heights on the banks of the Hudson River in September 1777. American general Schuyler had been fired for letting Burgoyne take Ticonderoga, and he had been replaced by General Horatio Gates and General Benedict Arnold...two commanders who totally hated each other's guts.

Gates had about seven thousand troops entrenched in a huge fort at the top of Bemis Heights. The Americans had been building this thing for weeks, and with the help of a super-genius Polish engineer named Tadeusz Kosciuszko, it was an impressive base of operations. Gates was happy to sit back there and dare Burgoyne to attack. But Benedict Arnold (the hero of the Canada invasion in chapter 5) hated the idea of waiting for the British to surround them and fire 138 cannons at their base. He wanted to attack. These two argued about this a *lot*, until finally Gates said, "Fine, do what you want with your half of the army, but I'm keeping my half here in this awesome fort."

On September 19, 1777, Gentleman Johnny ordered his most heroic general, Simon Fraser, to take a group of troops and capture a farm that was near Bemis Heights.

Unfortunately for Fraser, that position was being held by another guy you might remember from chapter 5: Big Daniel Morgan, the humongous Virginian who was missing half his teeth and had basically challenged the entire city of Quebec to a sword fight.

Daniel Morgan, c. 1794, painted by Charles Willson Peale

After spending some time as a prisoner of the British, Morgan was released in 1777. He immediately went to work creating a group of soldiers known as Morgan's Rangers. Consisting of five hundred men, most of them Scots-Irish and German, Morgan's unit was one of the first to make you pass a test to join: He would draw life-sized pictures of British officers (including King George III, by some accounts), and he'd only take you into the Rangers if you could hit one with a rifle from a hundred yards. He had all his men equipped with Pennsylvania long rifles, which were far more accurate (but took a lot longer to load) than British muskets. His men were so hardcore that Continental soldiers joked that for target practice these guys would shoot apples off each other's heads. Today, the United States Army Rangers trace their heritage to Morgan's company in the Revolution.

So when Morgan's crew popped up out of the farm's tall grass and opened fire into the British column, the enemy felt it. In a bloody, brutal engagement, Morgan's men drilled the British, killing dozens of officers and men. The British charged with bayonets, but accurate fire from Morgan's rifles cut them down. Before long, both armies were hurling more and more men into the fight, and a little skirmish over the farm became a huge gunfight between two armies.

Suddenly, out of nowhere, Benedict Arnold rode screaming up to the front lines, bringing his entire detachment. As the British lines faltered under the onslaught, Arnold sent a messenger telling Gates that this was it: "We have them, just attack!" But Gates refused. The British regrouped and held their ground, and then a huge counterattack forced Arnold to retreat. When Arnold got back to base, Gates yelled at him for almost losing the battle. Arnold got super-amazingly angry, and Gates stripped him of his command.

Not a lot happened for the next two weeks. At the bottom of the heights, Gentleman Johnny started building trenches and ramparts and moved all his cannons into position for an attack. Every day he sent a messenger or two to New York City to request help to attack these Americans from the rear. Atop the hill, the Americans just sat in their base, kicking back while more and more minutemen joined them every day. Meanwhile, American soldiers and raiders kept attacking supply lines from Ticonderoga, hammering every caravan of food and ammo before it could get to Burgoyne and the British.

In early October, Gentleman Johnny got some really, really bad news. Help from New York City wasn't coming. With winter setting in, his men getting cranky from all the cold weather and marching, more rebels showing up every day, and food supplies running out, Burgoyne had to act fast. Every day that passed brought him closer to defeat.

He decided to attack. He didn't realize that at this point he was actually pretty badly outnumbered by the rebels at the top of the hill.

On October 7, 1777, Burgoyne sent General Fraser around the side of the Americans to try to trick them into doing something foolish.

Once again, Fraser ran into Daniel Morgan.

Morgan had seen the British coming, and he snuck his Rangers through a wheat field to ambush them. His snipers hit hard and accurately, killing Fraser and many of his senior officers. The British attempted a brave bayonet charge, but Morgan's troops fought it off, and before long the British were being pushed back to their own fortifications.

At the top of Bemis Heights, General Benedict Arnold watched the fighting with wide-open eyes. Even though Gates had banned him from the battlefield and Arnold had no men to command, Arnold knew that this was the moment when the battle would be won or lost. Without any orders or any soldiers, he ran out to help.

Hessian and British forces were falling back in disarray, diving into a six-foot-deep trench they'd dug out of the earth. American soldiers, in their regular clothes, ran forward, waving knives, swinging their rifles, or firing point-blank into the enemy. Men everywhere were in hand-to-hand combat, punching and shooting.

Then, out of nowhere, General Benedict Arnold leapt his horse over a wooden wall, waving his sword and screaming for his men to follow him.

Fifty guys followed into a narrow gap between the British

lines. As enemy troops tried desperately to shoot him down from every direction, the American general led his men around behind the British and leapt feetfirst into another trench. Benedict Arnold was shot in the leg but continued to fight.

Then his horse took a bullet and fell, landing hard on Arnold's leg, which had now been shot twice. Arnold was pinned under his horse, his leg shattered, but still he called for his men to rally around him. The British line was broken, and General Johnny Burgoyne knew he'd lost the battle.

He ordered his entire army to abandon their trenches and retreat toward Canada.

When Burgoyne reached the nearby town of Saratoga, he received grim news from his scouts: Every road back to Canada was blocked by American militia forces. He was completely surrounded.

On October 16, 1777, Gentleman Johnny Burgoyne surrendered his entire army. Five thousand, eight hundred and ninety-five British, Hessian, and Canadian soldiers laid down their weapons.

> The courage and obstinacy with which the Americans fought were to the astonishment of everyone, and we now became fully convinced that they are not that contemptible enemy we had hitherto imagined them, incapable of standing in a regular engagement.
>
> —Lieutenant Thomas Anbury,
> British Twenty-Fourth Regiment
> of Foot

TADEUSZ KOSCIUSZKO

After the American Revolution, Polish engineer Tadeusz Kosciuszko (whom you might sometimes see referred to as "Thaddeus" Kosciuszko) returned home to the Polish-Lithuanian Commonwealth, only to find it at war with the Russian Empire of Empress Catherine the Great. Kosciuszko personally led a peasant uprising against the Russians, building an army of thousands, and led an infantry attack on the Russian garrison at Warsaw. The Poles fought bravely, but eventually Kosciuszko's uprising was crushed. He remained a prisoner of the empress until her death in 1796. Nowadays he is a national hero in Poland and Lithuania, and most major cities in Poland have streets or plazas named in his honor.

SET YOUR DECODER RINGS

Burgoyne and General Henry Clinton sent coded messages to each other using a spy technique called a "mask letter." Basically, one of them would write a big, long letter that didn't make a whole lot of sense. He would send it to the other guy, and that guy would place a special cutout over the letter. This cutout would block all the meaningless words and show only what the letter was actually supposed to say. Only Burgoyne and Clinton had the decoder cutouts, so if a letter was stolen by a rebel spy, that guy would have a hard time figuring out what the letter was all about.

Know Your Founding Fathers

NAME: Daniel Morgan

BIRTHDAY: July 6, 1736

BIRTHPLACE: Hunterdon County, New Jersey

CLAIM TO FAME: One of the toughest commanders of the American Revolution

JOB BEFORE THE WAR: Teamster and farmer

ROLE IN THE WAR: Commanded riflemen at the Battles of Quebec City, Saratoga, and Cowpens

AFTER THE WAR: Served in the US House of Representatives from 1797 to 1799

BONUS FACT: It's said that Morgan's cousin was frontiersman Daniel Boone (DNA evidence has since disproved this), and that his great-great-uncle was the famous British pirate Henry Morgan (also completely unproven). On the flip side, Civil War cavalry officer John Hunt Morgan claimed to be a direct descendant of Daniel Morgan, although—you guessed it—that's probably not true, either.

Valley Forge

Von Steuben Forges an Army

Valley Forge, Pennsylvania
February–May 1778

> Never before, or since, have I had such an impression of the ancient fabled God of War as when I looked on the baron. He seemed to me a perfect personification of Mars. The trappings of his horse, the enormous holsters of his pistols, his large size, and his strikingly martial aspect, all seemed to favor the idea.
>
> —Private Ashbel Green, New Jersey Militia

THE WINTER OF 1778 WAS ONE OF THE MOST freezing, miserable, please-god-just-end-it winters that has ever been recorded. In the snow-covered wasteland of Valley Forge, Pennsylvania, the men of the Continental Army were exhausted, unable to feel any sensations below the waist, and ready to give up after months of getting shanked in the face by Scottish Highlanders. They were suffering from sickness, starvation, hypothermia, and their bum knees acting up because they had to march twenty miles through the snow uphill both ways anytime they wanted a handful of week-old soup.

Their clothes, battered by long months of combat, were shredded to tatters and kind of looked like the rags you see zombies or werewolves wear in the movies. Many men were barefoot, their shoes either fallen apart or eaten for food. This was a scene that would make even the most nightmarish Boy Scout camp-out look like a weekend at Walt Disney World. One-third of the soldiers were listed as inactive due to illness. Some men simply dropped dead, while others peaced out, quit the war, and walked off the job. The rest struggled to survive through the winter cold, knowing that the only thing they had to look forward to was re-forming in the spring and getting kicked in the head by a powerful, invincible British Army that had just beat their pants off in huge battles around New York City and Philadelphia.

As the great revolutionary propaganda writer Thomas Paine put it in his appropriately named pamphlet *The American Crisis*: "These are the times that try men's souls."

But then, suddenly, in the midst of this frozen nightmare realm there appeared a sight that was so over-the-top bizarre that nobody knew what to make of it.

Through a driving blizzard on February 23, 1778, a convoy

of crazy Santa Claus–style sleighs blasted through the snow, pulled by a team of powerful, hard-charging black horses. Seated in the lead sleigh, surrounded by his servants, assistants, translators, a personal cook, and his pet greyhound, was a gigantic, barrel-chested, grizzled monster of a warrior. Decked out in a pristine officer's jacket from the Prussian Army of Frederick the Great, he was covered from shoulder to shoulder in gleaming medals. His scarred-up iron jaw was locked tight as he grimly checked out the sad lot of wannabe soldiers.

As the sleigh came to a stop, he calmly stepped off, his knee-high, well-polished black jackboots crunching the snow with the authority of a Dark Lord of the Sith. Slung by his side he wore two brass-plated, blinged-out flintlock pistols and a rad longsword that had been given to him by the Grand Duke of Hohenzollern-Hechingen in the German state of Swabia. His giant hand held a letter from Benjamin Franklin, introducing him as a military genius personally recommended by the French minister of war to aid the Colonial Army.

This was (get ready for another long name) Lieutenant General Friedrich Wilhelm Ludolf Gerhard Augustin, Freiherr von Steuben, Grand Marshal to the Prince of Swabia, and now major general in the Colonial Army. He'd been sent by Congress to drill this sorry group of farmer-soldiers into an elite fighting force.

Of course, while he did know how to make a pretty amazing

entrance, there are three very interesting things worth mentioning when we talk about Lieutenant General Baron von
Steuben: He wasn't really a baron, he wasn't really a general,
and he didn't speak a word of English.

But none of this stopped him from accomplishing his mission.

Friedrich von Steuben was born September 17, 1730,
in a cool-looking medieval German fortress castle called
Magdeburg. Friedrich's grandfather Augustin Steuben was
some random traveling preacher. But I guess he got tired of
being an ordinary guy, so he changed his named to Augustin
von Steuben and told everyone he was descended from an
ancient line of German barons. Nobody bothered to fact-check
this, and Augustin's son, Wilhelm, was able to use this fake
title to get an officer's commission in the Prussian military.

Wilhelm was an army engineer under Frederick the Great
(one of the most brilliant military geniuses in European history), and he was so good at building bridges and siege weaponry that he ended up receiving tons of high-ranking medals
for his bravery in battle. He even received the Blue Max,
the Prussian version of the Medal of Honor. As a young boy,
Friedrich traveled around on campaigns with his dad. After
seeing epic battles in Russia and Austria at his father's side,
Friedrich finally enlisted in the Prussian infantry at the age
of seventeen.

Like I said, though, von Steuben was never a general—in

fact, he was never higher than a captain, which is like a half dozen ranks below general. He served as a rifleman during the Seven Years' War (remember, it's the French and Indian War here in the United States), fought in the first and second Battles of Prague, survived a year in a Russian prisoner of war camp, and stood his ground against cavalry charges from epic French cuirassiers (look it up). As a first lieutenant in the elite Mayr Free Battalion, he led the attack at the Battle of Rossbach, running head-on into the enemy even though he was outnumbered two to one.

In 1762, von Steuben was promoted to captain and became a member of Frederick the Great's headquarters staff. There he helped manage a sixty-thousand-man army involved in epic battles across Europe. Von Steuben was personally trained by Frederick the Great, and when the Seven Years' War ended, von Steuben left the army, headed to the German state of Hohenzollern-Hechingen (no idea how you pronounce that) and spent twelve years as the Grand Marshal there.

Well, years passed, and in 1776, Baron von Steuben was bored, he was out of money, and his chief rival in the palace was telling everyone he should be fired. So, ticked off and ready for a new adventure, von Steuben packed his bags, went to Paris, and offered his services to Benjamin Franklin, who was in town to persuade the French to help the Americans out (more about this in the next chapter). Franklin looked at the baron's resume, basically *misread* the poorly translated phrase "Lieutenant, General Staff of Frederick the Great" as "Lieutenant General, Staff of Frederick the Great," and was like, "Heck yeah, dude, catch a ship to the colonies and let Congress know what's up." The next thing you know, this random fake Prussian general was shelling out his own cash to buy a fancy sleigh and servants so he could make an epic entrance at Valley Forge.

But here's where it gets good. Even though von Steuben *was not* a lot of things, he *was* a lifelong soldier with more combat experience in his sword arm than a *World of Warcraft* long-play YouTube walk-through. He'd survived the winter of 1759 in the frozen forests of Poland, almost starving along with fifty thousand half-frozen Prussian soldiers. He had shrapnel lodged in his body in several places, he'd been hit in the head with a sword, and he could run through intense military drills on his way to the bathroom. He took one look at this ragtag band of American patriots, said, "No European army could have held together in such circumstances," and started hardening these backwoods farmers into a razor-sharp spear of liberty.

He did this by personally standing in the knee-deep snow in full dress uniform with a rifle, single-handedly showing the men how to work their weapons and then swearing at them like a drill sergeant every time they messed up.

Drills started before dawn, and Baron von Steuben ran these demoralized American troops through the first boot camp in US history. Screaming and swearing like something out of an R-rated movie, von Steuben would start cursing in German, switch to French, and then start making up colorful new swearwords in broken English. When he ran out of curses, he would snap his fingers, and his assistant would come running and start screaming in English. Drills took place twice a day and were designed to teach the men to march in lockstep, load their rifles quickly, fight off bayonet attacks, and beat people up in hand-to-hand combat.

It might sound insane, but Baron von Steuben was actually

**Baron Friedrich von Steuben, 1780,
painted by Charles Willson Peale**

massively popular with the soldiers he was shouting at. For starters, the major general actually *did* the drills with his men, which was unheard of at the time. British officers believed it was "ungentlemanly" to get down and dirty, so they never did this. And as for the screaming and swearing, men would show up to watch the drills just to marvel at this guy's ridiculous vocabulary of profanity. Also, von Steuben made a point of learning the name of every soldier in the army. After he was done hammering them into soldiers, he built them back up to have pride in their abilities. This is the same strategy used in basic training across the US military today.

Two things that von Steuben really focused on were loading muskets and fighting with bayonets. The Americans had always been tough fighters, but von Steuben was appalled by how long it took these guys to load their rifles. So all day every day, he had his men go through the procedure of loading and firing a musket. They didn't actually shoot them—they didn't have enough ammo to waste—but after a while they could prime the powder, ram a musket ball, and fire in their sleep.

He also was enraged when he heard stories of how the Americans were terrified of British bayonet charges. Von Steuben collected every bayonet he could find (a bunch of them were just starting to be imported from France) and taught these guys how to parry and take enemies out by jabbing them in the torso. By the time he was done, the

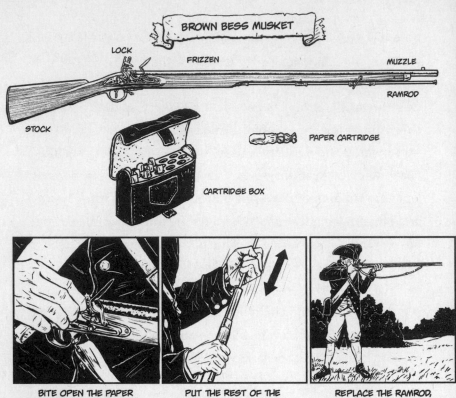

BROWN BESS MUSKET

LOCK

FRIZZEN

MUZZLE

RAMROD

STOCK

PAPER CARTRIDGE

CARTRIDGE BOX

BITE OPEN THE PAPER CARTRIDGE AND PRIME THE FRIZZEN WITH A LITTLE GUNPOWDER.

PUT THE REST OF THE CARTRIDGE IN THE MUZZLE, AND USE THE RAMROD TO PUSH THE CARTRIDGE DOWN THE BARREL.

REPLACE THE RAMROD, ENGAGE THE LOCK, AND PREPARE TO FIRE!

Americans could march, wheel, fire by company, reload twice as fast as before, and then charge into the enemy with bayonets.

It took him four months to make the sad group of guys from the beginning of the chapter into an army that could strike fear into the heart of the British.

Von Steuben eventually wrote his instructions down (in French), and they were translated into English by Continental commanders Alexander Hamilton and Nathanael Greene. Known originally as "Baron Steuben's Instructions," the text was eventually renamed "Regulations for the Order and Discipline of the Troops of the United States." It was used by the US Army until 1814.

Another important accomplishment of von Steuben was that he got the camp at Valley Forge whipped into shape as well. He ordered everybody to clean their rooms, take out the trash, and scrub the bathrooms. He kept track of supplies and demanded monthly inspections of equipment stores, and any guy who failed to keep his rifle shipshape found himself getting kicked with a Prussian jackboot. His efforts reduced disease in the camp, and by the time he wrote his last camp report in May 1778, there were only three muskets in the entire Continental Army that were listed as "deficient."

The British had ended the campaigns of 1777 by crushing the Continental Army at the Battles of Brandywine and Germantown. They'd smashed George Washington's troops with imperial discipline and the tip of the bayonet and had captured Philadelphia. But when the redcoats encountered that same army in the spring of 1778, they faced a very different group of soldiers, and the difference shocked the British Army to its core.

The summer soldier and the sunshine patriot
   will, in this crisis,
shrink from the service of their country; but he
   that stands it now,
deserves the love and thanks of man and woman.
Tyranny, like hell, is not easily conquered;
yet we have this consolation with us,
that the harder the conflict, the more glorious
   the triumph.

—**Thomas Paine,** *The American Crisis*

VON STEUBEN DAY

Nowadays, September 17 is known as Von Steuben Day in the United States. It's a pretty big deal to German-Americans, but for an old guy like me, it's probably best known as the parade where Ferris Bueller sings "Danke Schoen" in the tremendous 1986 film *Ferris Bueller's Day Off.*

THE WOMEN OF VALLEY FORGE

There were a number of women at Valley Forge, suffering equally through that horrible winter of death, disease, and freezing temperatures. Men were allowed to bring their wives to stay with them, which many did, and other women prepared food, mended uniforms, created ammunition, and did laundry. Some women made eight dollars a month working as nurses. Even George Washington's wife, Martha, came to spend the winter, helping her husband organize the camp and officers' barracks. In a situation as bleak as Valley Forge, many men wrote home to their families saying that it was comforting to have so many compassionate, inspirational women working to keep the army running.

The Badge of Military Merit

On August 7, 1782, George Washington approved the creation of a Medal of Military Merit, to be given to enlisted men who performed heroic acts in battle. The medal was in the shape of a heart, trimmed with purple ribbon, and the men who received it would be allowed to wear it proudly on their uniform. We only know three men who received this honor, and after the Revolution pretty much everybody forgot about it. However, in 1932 (what would have been Washington's two hundredth birthday), US Secretary of War Douglas MacArthur brought the award back into service with the military. Today we know it as the Purple Heart, and it is awarded to any US military personnel killed or wounded in service of the country.

Know Your Founding Fathers

NAME: Friedrich Wilhelm Ludolf Gerhard Augustin von Steuben

BIRTHDAY: September 17, 1730

BIRTHPLACE: Magdeburg, Prussia (Germany)

CLAIM TO FAME: Drillmaster of the Continental Army

JOB BEFORE THE WAR: Captain in the Prussian Army

ROLE IN THE WAR: Inspector general in charge of the drill and preparation of American troops

AFTER THE WAR: Retired, moved to the New York countryside

BONUS FACT: In the 2003 PBS Kids cartoon series *Liberty's Kids*, von Steuben was voiced by Arnold Schwarzenegger.

Courting France

Negotiating a French-American Alliance

Paris, France
July 7, 1776–May 4, 1778

> [France is] the dominant power of Europe, being incomparably the most powerful at land, that united in a close alliance with our states, and enjoying the benefit of our trade, there is not the smallest reason to doubt but both will be a sufficient curb upon the naval power of Great Britain.

—John Adams

THE CONTINENTAL CONGRESS FELT PRETTY awesome about itself after signing the Declaration of Independence in 1776. But just because you *say* you're a country doesn't mean you actually *are* one. If that were the case, every crazy person out there could raise a flag over his house and say he doesn't want to pay taxes because he wants to be his own country. No, to be accepted as a new country, you need to be officially recognized by other countries and set up trade deals and diplomatic relations. And that's not the easiest thing to do when you're a king-hating free society of Protestant rebels trying to split away from the richest and most powerful military force on Earth.

So it was very clear from a really early point that America wasn't going to win a war against England all by itself. The Americans needed allies, money, extra troops, and equipment. They needed military alliances with other powerful European countries so that Britain would be battling multiple enemies at once—not focusing its might solely on America.

For many delegates at the Continental Congress, the most obvious choice for help was the Kingdom of France, the same country that had just fought a war *against* the American colonists ten years earlier. France had been humiliated by England in the Seven Years' War, but the kingdom was still wealthy and powerful, had a fairly decent navy, and was looking for a good opportunity to get revenge.

And don't forget about the Marquis de Lafayette. From the moment he'd landed in the New World, he had been sending letters home to the king asking for aid, weapons, and money to help in the war. But this wasn't always effective. So three days after signing the Declaration of Independence, the Continental Congress sent a man named Silas Deane to Paris to try to negotiate with the French government. Deane did all right, but it didn't help that his personal secretary turned out to be a British spy. Or that Deane was later arrested and charged with taking money from the Continental Congress and the French government and putting it straight into his personal bank account (he swore he was innocent but never got a chance to prove it).

So the Continental Congress sent two more men in December 1776 to join the negotiating team: a Virginia doctor named Arthur Lee, and famous Philadelphian Benjamin Franklin.

As I mentioned back in chapter 6, Ben Franklin was a superstar celebrity in 1776. Now seventy years old, he had been born in Boston, had written dozens of books, had spent twenty-five years running the world-famous magazine *Poor Richard's Almanack*, had invented a cast-iron fireplace known as the Franklin stove, and had been one of the first people to study the electrical power of lightning (in an insane experiment where he flew a kite in a thunderstorm). Franklin had spent most of his life in Philadelphia, where he'd built a library, established a fire department, and founded the University of Pennsylvania. Franklin was fluent in French, and the people of France welcomed him.

Franklin, Deane, and Lee did not have an easy job ahead of them. Sure, France wanted to break up the ultra-powerful British Empire, but they weren't pumped about a powerful United States of America, either. First off, America was

Benjamin Franklin, 1767, painted by David Martin

overthrowing a king, and the French king didn't want his citizens or the other French colonies to follow America's lead. Second, the French were Catholics, and America was a pretty solidly Protestant country. This was a big deal because people used to kill each other in the streets over stuff like that back in the day.

Then there was the whole thing about actually trying to take on England in a fight. The French had half as many warships as England, and their army had just been worked over by the Brits ten years earlier. If the American Revolution failed, England would turn its full might against France again…and that would be very, very bad for the country. So, at first, France was polite, but the French king wasn't super-excited about sending men to die for a cause just so he could possibly weaken the British Empire. Dr. Arthur Lee got a similar answer from a Spanish diplomat in Victoria, Spain, in 1777. "Sure, the Spanish would love to see England fall, but the king secretly hopes your revolution fails. He doesn't want you to inspire his people or his colonies to revolt and try to set up their own democracies."

None of this discouraged the Americans, and they were able to find a few friends among the regular folks of France. The most important one was a businessman named Pierre de Beaumarchais, a watchmaker who'd invented a new type of timekeeping mechanism. Then he quit his job to become a spy in London and Vienna, then quit that job to become a playwright (he wrote *The Barber of Seville* and *The Marriage of Figaro*). He also made super-expensive business deals on the side. No bigs.

Beaumarchais hated kings, liked personal freedoms, and was really popular in the French court, and he agreed to help Franklin and the Americans in their struggle for liberty. So Beaumarchais set up Rodrigue Hortalez and Company, which, on the surface, was just a regular merchant ship business. But in reality, Beaumarchais borrowed $200,000 from the French government and $200,000 from the Spanish government, bought a bunch of ships and guns, and started running a trade route to smuggle weapons to the American Revolution. In early 1777, Beaumarchais's fleet of merchant ships landed in the colonies with thousands of French muskets, thousands of bayonets, two hundred cannons, hundreds of tons of gunpowder, and enough uniforms for twenty-five thousand Continental soldiers. It's said that 90 percent of the gunpowder used by American forces at the Battle of Saratoga came from this shipment.

By the end of the war, Beaumarchais's company had expanded to forty ships, sailing under the escort of French warships. In just five years, Hortalez and Company delivered $62 million worth of equipment, then came back to France with enough American sugar, spices, tobacco, rice, and cotton to make a profit.

But still the Americans needed more. They needed assistance from the French Navy and the French Army to take down Great Britain. And in 1777, they got a huge break. When news of the epic victory in the Battle of Saratoga reached Europe, the British panicked. King George sent a negotiator named Paul Wentworth to Paris to meet with Franklin, Lee, and Deane. He offered tons of money, high government positions, and fancy houses to the Americans if they would just agree to sign a peace treaty with England and end the war.

Franklin, a hardcore advocate of American freedom, smiled, politely declined, then walked straight over to the French diplomats and told them Britain had just offered the

Americans a treaty. The French, seeing that America had really scared England into thinking it could lose the war, were like, "No, wait, we can do this, give us a chance." And on February 6, 1778, the king of France signed the Treaty of Alliance with the United States of America. Under the treaty, France would get trading privileges with the United States in exchange for military support. Anything the French captured in North America would go to the Americans, but anything they captured in the rest of the world they could keep after the war.

When British spies reported the deal to the king of England, he got *reeeeeeeeally* nervous. He sent the Earl of Carlisle to America on an official mission with a very favorable offer:

"If you agree to end the war now, we will give you everything you wanted. You'll have seats in Parliament. We'll repeal the taxes you didn't like. You name it."

The Continental Congress heard Carlisle's offer, nodded their heads, and basically told him, "If you'd presented this offer to us two years ago we would have jumped at it. But you didn't, and now it's too late. Independence or nothing."

On March 17, 1778, the British Empire declared war on France. Spain joined the war on the side of France and America almost immediately.

The American Revolution had just gotten a whole lot more interesting. And more global.

MAKING FRIENDS ISN'T EASY

Spain and France weren't the only two countries visited by American diplomats. The Continental Congress also sent delegates to Holland, Prussia, Russia, and a few other places, but with limited success. The poor guy who went to Russia had to stand outside Catherine the Great's palace in the dead of winter for four hours before she agreed to meet with him! Holland joined the America-France-Spain alliance in 1780, contributing money and ships to the Revolution. But the other nations refused to recognize the United States as a country until the war ended in 1783.

THE WORLD AT WAR

This book mostly focuses on the events of the American Revolution that took place in North America, but it was truly a world war that caused death and destruction on multiple continents. In the Caribbean, France captured the British islands of Grenada, Montserrat, Saint Vincent, Tobago, and Saint Kitts. But a naval defeat at the Battle of the Saintes in 1782 prevented them from capturing Jamaica. France also led attacks on the British holdings in India, but the British infantry forces crushed them. The Spanish, led by Bernardo de Gálvez, overran British holdings in present-day Alabama, Mississippi, and Florida, and Spanish fleets also attacked British bases in South America.

In a weird turn of events, the biggest battle of the war was actually the Great Siege of Gibraltar. A combined French and Spanish fleet sent nearly forty thousand soldiers to capture the British fort at Gibraltar on the southern tip of Spain. The heroic British defenders held out for *three years* (!!!) straight, using eight thousand barrels' worth of gunpowder to drive off their enemies. Even with victories such as this, however, the British were forced to divert more and more troops, money, ships, and supplies away from the war with the Americans.

Know Your Founding Fathers

NAME: Benjamin Franklin

BIRTHDAY: January 17, 1706

BIRTHPLACE: Boston, Massachusetts

CLAIM TO FAME: World-famous author and inventor, international celebrity

JOB BEFORE THE WAR: Author, inventor, printer, scientist, postmaster, politician

ROLE IN THE WAR: Delegate in the Second Continental Congress; helped write the Declaration of Independence; led the delegations that negotiated the treaty with France and the treaty that ended the war

AFTER THE WAR: US minister to France from 1778 to 1785; governor of Pennsylvania from 1785 to 1788

BONUS FACT: Ben Franklin's son William was the governor of New Jersey during the war, but William was a hardcore loyalist who didn't think America should break away from England. Franklin and his son got into such a big argument over independence that the two men never spoke to each other again.

The Legend of Molly Pitcher

The Battle of Monmouth

Monmouth, New Jersey
June 28, 1778

A woman whose husband belonged to the artillery and who was then attached to a piece in the engagement, attended with her husband at the piece for the whole time. While in the act of reaching a cartridge and having one of her feet as far before the other as she could step, a cannon shot from the enemy passed directly between her legs without doing any other damage than carrying away all the lower part of her petticoat. Looking at it with apparent unconcern, she observed that it was lucky it did not pass a little higher, for in that case it might have carried away something else, and continued her occupation.

—Private Joseph Plumb Martin, Seventeenth Continental Regiment

I N 1778, WORRIES ABOUT A FRENCH NAVAL
attack on New York City marked the beginning of a new
phase of the war for Great Britain. General William Howe,
the British commander up until this point, was fired, and he
was replaced by General Henry Clinton, the guy who had led
the attacks at Brooklyn and Brandywine (major British victories). Clinton was immediately ordered to bring his army back
from Philadelphia to New York to defend that city, which was
not a small thing to ask. This dude was now supposed to move
19,500 men and hundreds of wagons across three states that
were completely filled with rebel militia trying to kill him.

On the American side, George Washington had a whole new
army under his command as the snow melted at Valley Forge.
They were highly trained, equipped with top-of-the-line gear,
and ready for a fight. Washington's spies knew Clinton's plan
to get back to New York, and Washington wanted to hit the
British as soon as they turned their backs on him.

Now is probably a good time to talk about George
Washington's second-in-command, a guy named Charles Lee.
Lee was the most experienced American commander...but he
was basically useless. For instance, shortly after the Battle of
Brooklyn, he actually got captured by British cavalry while he
was still in his underwear. Then, if that wasn't bad enough,
he sang like a canary when the Brits asked him for information on the American forces. It's not that Lee was a traitor

(although he was so dumb that many historians wonder if he actually was a British spy in disguise). It's just that he was really incompetent and only cared about being famous and important and having people think he was cool.

Charles Lee had been back with the Continental Army for only about a month at the start of this campaign, and he was totally against attacking the British as they retreated to New York City. He was like, "Nah, it's cool, let's just let them slip away even though we have the perfect opportunity to smash them." The Marquis de Lafayette and General "Mad" Anthony Wayne saw it differently. They wanted to strike, and Washington agreed. He gave half of his army to Lafayette and told him to hit the British outside the town of Monmouth, New Jersey.

Lee got super-mad, threw a temper tantrum, and started crying about how *he* should lead the attack because he was the most senior officer. So Washington gave him command.

Charles Lee, of course, messed it all up.

Two things worked against Lee at the Battle of Monmouth on June 28, 1778. The first was that he was lazy. He didn't bother to research the land or to figure out what was going on. He just ran in there blind, which is like trying to play a board game without actually knowing what the board looks like. The second thing that worked against Lee was that British commander Henry Clinton was totally expecting an attack at Monmouth. He had scouted the land and set

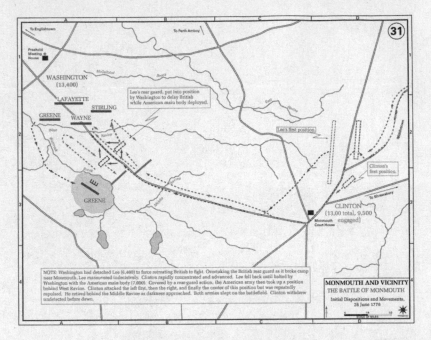

Map of the Battle of Monmouth

up an ingenious trap to destroy the Continental Army all at once.

It was around noon on June 28, 1778, when General Washington started hearing the sounds of gunfire and artillery *way* too close to his position at Valley Forge. He raced forward on his horse to check out what was going on, and when he reached the top of a nearby hill, he saw something horrible. Instead of his men crushing the British, he saw six thousand Americans running for their lives while the British shot at their backs. Only one unit, the soldiers under "Mad" Anthony

Wayne, stood their ground, taking horrific casualties and sacrificing their lives to buy time for the rest of the army to escape.

In that instant, George Washington became the most insanely angry human being on the planet.

You don't really think of Founding Fathers as being human beings. They seem...above it, like they're superheroes or something. Well, it's true that George Washington kind of was that way. He rarely used bad language, for instance. But when he stormed to the battlefront and found Charles Lee, he apparently shouted such a horrific barrage of R-rated words that it probably killed every flower in a ten-mile radius. It was a string of curse words so epic that the rant actually gets mentioned in a lot of history textbooks, and you know you've really ripped someone good if people are still talking about it two hundred years after it happened. Lee was immediately stripped of command, and Washington rode out at the front of the army, screaming for his men to follow him, form a line, and hold off the entire British Army.

Henry Knox had lost a good number of his cannons at Brandywine, but he rolled his guys up and had them run as fast as they could with their remaining cannons to the front lines. In the blazing, hundred-degree weather of the scorching New Jersey summer, men were dropping left and right from heat exhaustion. But they moved their guns, formed a wall, and started cranking fire into the enemy. With bullets whizzing past his head, Knox gave his men orders, helped drag ammo carts, and directed fire at charging cavalry.

At the front lines, a twenty-four-year-old New Jersey woman named Mary Ludwig Hays rushed forward, carrying a large, heavy pitcher of cold water she'd just picked up from the river. Around her shoulders were slung four hefty iron canteens, each holding about five pounds of water. This wasn't a weird sight to the men of the Revolutionary War—there were thousands of women who traveled with the army. They rarely fought (see chapter 18 for an exception to this), but they acted as nurses, helped carry supplies, cooked, and refilled stores of ammunition and water during battles. Sometimes they rode on horseback to pass information between commanders. Mary Ludwig Hays was attached to a cannon crew as an assistant, and her job was absolutely crucial. As the powder-blackened woman reached the cannon, she passed her canteens to the sweating, exhausted men (including her husband, John, who was a loader for the cannon). Then she poured her bucket of water along the red-hot barrel of the cannon, cooling it off so it wouldn't overheat and stop working.

Despite all the efforts of the cannon crews, the British pushed on. Henry Clinton, personally leading a cavalry charge, was shocked by the accuracy and damage of the American infantry. Truly, the training of von Steuben had paid off, and Clinton didn't know what to do about it. So he ordered another charge.

Around this time, George Washington looked up at the hill where Knox's cannons were stationed, and he was amazed to see a woman working on one of the guns. Carrying a large ramrod, her face and petticoat blackened and singed, she ignored bullets and cannonballs exploding around her as she helped to load the large cannon and keep it firing. Around her, several members of her crew were down on the ground, either wounded or passed out from the oppressive heat. At one point a cannonball passed right by her, so close it nearly killed her, but Mary Ludwig Hays wasn't about to give up

just because she'd nearly had her midsection exploded by a twelve-pound chunk of iron. She just continued cleaning out the barrel, pouring in the powder, loading a cannonball, and firing the gun, and doing an impressive job of it.

The Continental Army formed up in a line and rallied around Generals Washington and Knox. Despite bayonet charges, cavalry attacks, and full-on assaults by the British, the American forces continued to fight heroically, pouring out cannon and rifle fire that threw every attack backward. As darkness fell, General Clinton ordered the British to withdraw and continue their retreat to New York City. They would not destroy Washington's army today.

After the battle, the men of Mary Hays's cannon crew rallied around their new heroine. As stories got out to the newspapers across the colonies, she was given a new nickname, Molly Pitcher, because of the water she brought the men during the fighting. She ended up being an inspiration to people across the country. She and her husband both finished out the war as part of the cannon crew, and she became one of the only women of the Revolution to receive a military veteran's pension after the fighting was over.

YOU PICKED THE WRONG HOUSE, FELLAS

Another tough-as-heck Revolutionary War woman was a North Carolina frontierswoman named Nancy Hart. A distant cousin of Daniel Morgan (the rifleman from Saratoga and Quebec City), Hart was tough, tall, and an expert hunter and survivalist. She also had a scarred-up face and didn't look like the sort of person you'd want to mess with. Well, one day a group of six loyalist soldiers came to her cabin and demanded that she cook them up some dinner. Hart gritted her teeth and cooked a turkey, and the loyalists all stacked their (loaded) rifles by the door and sat down at her table. Once they'd started eating, Hart ran to the stack of rifles, grabbed one, pointed it at the men, and told them to surrender. One loyalist started walking toward her, so she blew him away. Another guy tried to overpower her, but she grabbed another loaded rifle and fragged him, too. The rest of the guys surrendered, and she marched them off to the militia as prisoners of war.

GOOD MORNING, CAPTAIN MOLLY!

A lot of people get confused because there are actually two Molly Pitcher stories from the American Revolution. The second story is the tale of Margaret Corbin, a heroine who fought at the Battle of Fort Washington in 1776. When Margaret's husband was killed while working his cannon, Corbin rushed up to the gun and took his spot, firing a blast into a swarm of Hessian bayonets. She worked the gun, firing over and over, until a British blast of grapeshot ripped into her chest and nearly blew her arm off. But Corbin survived, served through the rest of the war, and also became one of the few women to receive a pension from the US Army. In her later years, this bad-tempered, hard-drinking woman could often be seen wearing her Continental Army jacket around her hometown. When men saw her, they would salute and say, "Good morning, Captain Molly!"

Know Your Founding Fathers (and Mothers!)

NAME: Mary Ludwig Hays

BIRTHDAY: October 13, 1754

BIRTHPLACE: Trenton, New Jersey

CLAIM TO FAME: Fired a cannon during the Battle of Monmouth

JOB BEFORE THE WAR: Housewife; camp follower

ROLE IN THE WAR: Camp follower and artillerist

AFTER THE WAR: She left the army as a sergeant and moved to Carlisle, Pennsylvania, with her husband, John.

BONUS FACT: The state of Tennessee offers a special commemorative license plate to female veterans of the US Army. This plate features a picture of Molly Pitcher to commemorate the history of women soldiers' service to the US military.

"Mad" Anthony and the Virginia Hercules

The Battle of Stony Point
Stony Point, New York
July 16, 1779

Issue the orders, Sir, and I will storm Hell.

—General "Mad" Anthony Wayne,
Continental Army Light Corps

I'M GOING TO NEED VOLUNTEERS TO LEAD the assault," General "Mad" Anthony Wayne whispered to his men on the night of July 16, 1779. "The first man into the fort will receive five hundred dollars. The next four will get a hundred dollars each."

Crouching in ankle-deep water behind a thick line of bushes, the elite soldiers of the Continental Army Light Corps strained their eyes through the pitch-black sky at Fort

Stony Point, New York. It was barely lit by the torches of the British guards, but even in the dim blackness it was a pretty scary sight. Rising 150 feet above the Hudson River, Stony Point sat atop a steep, rocky cliff with water on three sides. The approach was treacherous—after wading through a river, crossing a swamp, and climbing up the uneven cliff, attackers then had to get past two abatises, which are like big rows of chopped-down trees with the ends whittled into spikes pointing in the direction of the enemy.

Both sets of walls were patrolled by imperial troops from the Seventy-First Highlanders Regiment, one of the toughest units of kilt-wearing, red-coated Scotsmen in the British Army. Beyond them were the stone walls of the fort, bristling with the barrels of nearly fifteen cannons. In the river below, the Americans could clearly see the sails of the HMS *Vulture*, a British sloop of war with an additional sixteen cannons. Inside the fort were an estimated six hundred to eight hundred British soldiers.

When General George Washington ordered the attack on Stony Point, he knew it would be a long shot. That's why he put the operation under the control of his most daring, most fearless general, "Mad" Anthony Wayne. That's also why he gave Wayne full command of the Light Corps, a handpicked group of veteran troops all personally trained by Baron Friedrich von Steuben and equipped with the best gear in the Continental Army. One by one, the men surveyed the

Anthony Wayne

situation, gritted their teeth, locked in their bayonets, and began stepping forward to volunteer.

After making it safely to New York, British commander Henry Clinton began working on a new plan of attack, since these upstart colonists were proving tougher than he'd hoped. His goal in 1779 was to capture the Hudson River, but that was easier said than done. Why? Because the most heavily defended position in North America at the time was a fort on the Hudson called West Point. West Point was known as "the Key to America" because of its importance, and Washington did everything he could to make it secure. Under the guidance of Tadeusz Kosciuszko (remember the Polish engineer from chapter 10?), the Americans had set up dozens of cannons and a huge chain across the Hudson River to block British ships.

Nevertheless, Clinton was determined to take the Hudson River. His first step on this mission was to capture Stony Point (which he did), which was just twelve miles south of West Point. Washington knew the British could use the fort at Stony Point as a base for their attack on West Point, so he called in "Mad" Anthony and the Light Corps to take it back. There wasn't time or manpower for a long siege, though, so this attack needed to be quick and decisive. Basically, it was quite possibly the first Special Operations attack ever undertaken by the American military.

"Mad" Anthony Wayne knew it was crazy. The night before the battle, he wrote a letter to his best friend back home in Pennsylvania. Basically, he said, "If anything happens to me, take care of my wife, my son, and my daughter. Let them know that I fought for the cause of freedom." He ended it by saying, "Tomorrow I shall eat dinner either inside the enemy's lines or in the other world."

The operation was so secret that even as they marched out on the night of July 16, 1779, the men of the Light Corps still had no idea where the heck they were going. Wayne led them fourteen miles through upstate New York, ducking through trees and bushes, marching through swamps, and sneaking closer until they were in sight of the fort. He told his men, "Fix bayonets, but do *not* load your guns. This is a stealth operation. It needs to be quiet, and if someone's rifle goes off by accident it could ruin the whole thing. So grab your knives, swords, and bayonets, and plan on using them first."

Luckily for "Mad" Anthony Wayne, he had one of the most unbelievably hardcore hand-to-hand fighters in the entire American army on his side that night. Sergeant Peter "the Virginia Hercules" Francisco was a behemoth of a man, standing well over six feet tall and towering over the other soldiers in the unit. In his gigantic hands, he was packing a huge broadsword, and his arms were jacked with the muscles needed to swing such a hefty weapon around.

Peter Francisco's story is a truly bizarre one. He first appeared in history on a foggy night in 1765, when he washed up on a quiet dock on the Virginia coast. Just five years old, this young boy spoke no English, had no idea where he came from, and had no recollection of how he'd arrived in the colonies. Honestly, to this day we still can only guess at where the heck he came from. Young Peter was taken in by a wealthy Virginia family (relatives of Patrick Henry, no less!) and he soon grew to be six feet six inches tall and 280 pounds at a time when the average American was about five feet seven inches tall! He was freakishly strong, made his living as a blacksmith, and performed cool feats of strength in his village, usually impressing all the girls by bench-pressing a wagon or wrestling an ox or something equally over-the-top. When the war started, he enlisted in the militia, and by 1779 he had survived two gunshot wounds, fought in several battles, and made it through the winter at Valley Forge, and once (according to legend, of course) dragged a cannon across a battlefield all by himself.

Naturally, a guy like that would be one of the first men to volunteer for the attack on Stony Point. Peter was placed in a small squad called "Forlorn Hope" (*forlorn* is a synonym for *hopeless*), which was what a lot of armies called suicide missions back in the eighteenth century. Basically, he would be in the first group to run headfirst into the enemy fort and start fighting anybody he found in there. After they'd spearheaded into the base, Wayne would personally lead the group that would follow them into the fight. They didn't call him "Mad" Anthony for nothing—they called him that because he *really loved fighting*.

The Light Corps maneuvered into position for the attack. Francisco's Forlorn Hope, led by a French-American lieutenant colonel named François-Louis de Fleury, headed straight toward the imposing fortress at the top of the hill, with Wayne's group backing them up. The men waded through the waist-deep water of a swamp, forded a river, scrambled up the hill to the south, and found really awesome hiding spots out of view of the British base.

While they did this, other detachments of Wayne's men headed into different positions around Stony Point to prepare their attacks as well. Once the trap was ready, a small group of Wayne's riflemen lined up across from the main gate of Stony

Point, took a deep breath, sighted their rifles at the fort, and unleashed a volley of sniper fire at the guards on the walls.

Then things got *really* crazy.

Loyalist spies had warned the British commander of Stony Point that an attack might be coming. Lieutenant Colonel Henry Johnson had ordered his men to sleep in their uniforms that night, and *the second* the gunshots began to ring out, these men hopped up, grabbed their gear, and started rushing to position. Johnson, in the middle of all the confusion, took Wayne's bait—he thought the small group of guys shooting at the gate was actually the main attack. So while the main American force hid in the darkness, Johnson formed up his infantry, fixed bayonets, and went running out the front door to attack.

Then, out of the darkness, the American forces rose up and rushed forward, bayonets and swords at the ready. Some of them smashed into the flank of Johnson's attack. Others ran straight through the wide-open doors of the fort itself.

The darkness of the battlefield was lit only by flashes of musket or cannon fire that rippled all through Stony Point, creating an insane amount of confusion on both sides. British cannon crews fired at their own men in some places and mistakenly identified Wayne's men as friendly troops in others. Complete chaos swirled as armies crashed into each other in the darkness, shooting, punching, biting, and stabbing in an epic action-movie brawl.

"Mad" Anthony Wayne and François-Louis de Fleury ran for

the main gates, which had been left open by Johnson's charge. British troops opened fire on them immediately, ripping into the Americans with a barrage of bullets. Wayne was struck in the head by a musket ball, falling hard to the ground. With the world spinning around him and blood pouring down his face, "Mad" Anthony screamed, *"Forward, my brave fellows, forward! Victory is already in your hands!"* Then, as his aides ran to treat his injury, he calmly whispered to them, *"If I am fatally injured, carry me into the fort, and let me die there in triumph."*

At the head of the column, Forlorn Hope, led by Lieutenant Colonel de Fleury and Sergeant Peter Francisco, pounded at a dead sprint into the courtyard of Fort Stony Point. The British opened fire, unloading a volley straight into the American assault, but still the Colonial troops stormed ahead. The defenders didn't have time to reload, so they lowered their bayonets, belted out a battle cry, and charged forward for some old-school, medieval-style sword fighting.

Towering over everyone in the courtyard, Peter Francisco made his humongous blade flash as he parried a bayonet and started swinging away at anything unlucky enough to be dressed in red. He personally killed three British soldiers in the courtyard, then stomped his way up a ladder toward the parapet. British soldiers were at the top of the walls, firing down on the patriots swarming into their base, but Francisco raced along the wall, throwing men off or cutting them down with the blade.

When he and de Fleury reached the main tower, they were swarmed by more redcoats. Francisco cut a couple down, but then a British officer slashed the Virginia Hercules hard across the chest. Bleeding profusely, Francisco totally Hulked out and bellowed with rage. His furious blows took out the officer and most of the people in that dude's general area. While this was going on, Lieutenant Colonel de Fleury, having emptied his pistols and bloodied his sword, pulled the British flag down from the flagpole.

When the British fighting on the walls and in the fort saw their colors torn from the fort, they assumed they had been overrun by a superior number of rebel soldiers. Most of the defenders immediately dropped their weapons and surrendered. "Mad" Anthony Wayne, bloodied but still conscious (you know, just a musket ball to the head, no big deal), ordered that no man who surrendered was to be harmed in any way. The fight was over pretty much immediately.

Against all odds, the fort was now his.

Sitting in the Hudson River, the British HMS *Vulture* could not see through the darkness that the British flag was no longer flying above the fort. When the crew of the *Vulture* heard a large cheer coming from the fort, they assumed the British had won, so the crew all cheered back and fired a celebratory volley from their cannons. So…you can probably imagine how surprised they were when a soaking-wet British dude swam all the way out to their ship to tell them that the fort had been taken by the enemy. Knowing that every gun in Stony Point would probably soon be pointed in their direction, the crew of the *Vulture* got the heck out of there as fast as their sails could carry them.

The Americans had 15 men dead and 83 wounded, but they had captured Stony Point and taken 543 British soldiers and officers prisoner in the process. Of the nineteen British killed at the Battle of Stony Point, Sergeant Peter Francisco has been credited with killing twelve of them himself. He received a hundred dollars for being the second man into the fort, immediately behind François-Louis de Fleury.

Every man who participated in the attack was basically a hero across America, effective immediately. "Mad" Anthony Wayne somehow survived being shot in the head, and he received a gold medal from the Continental Congress to reward him for his bravery. François-Louis de Fleury was awarded a silver medal and received the five-hundred-dollar bounty for being the first man in the fort. To this day, the US Army gives out an award called the De Fleury Medal every year to its best combat engineer.

LESSONS LEARNED

A few years before Stony Point, "Mad" Anthony Wayne survived a horrible nighttime bayonet attack of his own. Immediately after the American defeat at the Battle of Brandywine, Wayne's troops were ordered to keep an eye on the British movements. Well, Wayne's Pennsylvania infantry camped out a little too close to British lines, and in the middle of the night on September 20, 1777, a group of British dragoons and light infantry infiltrated his camp and started silently killing everyone with bayonets. The Americans woke up and tried to surrender, but the British still killed quite a few men even after they gave up. All told, the Americans had 53 dead, 113 wounded, and 71 captured. From that point on, Wayne decided on three things: Night attacks are confusing, bayonets are super-stealthy, and it's super-not-cool to kill people after they surrender.

Financing the Rebellion

One of the great unsung heroes of the American Revolution was a New York City merchant named Haym Salomon, the "financier of the Revolution." A Polish-born Jewish immigrant, Salomon was arrested by the British as a spy in 1776 and almost died during his imprisonment, but once the Brits learned that he spoke fluent English and German, he ended up working as an interpreter to help the redcoats talk to their Hessian mercenaries. While working for the British, Salomon not only convinced five hundred Hessian mercenaries to desert the army, he also helped a bunch of American prisoners escape from jail before he was released. In 1778, Salomon was arrested again and sentenced to be hanged as a traitor the next morning. But he escaped from prison *that same night*, fled New York, and traveled through enemy lines all the way to Philadelphia. In Philly, Salomon worked with Continental Congressman Robert Morris to set up a series of financial deals that helped America pay its soldiers, continue the war, and finance the new government. Salomon donated nearly $350,000 for the Revolution and is credited with saving the United States from complete economic collapse in the early years of the country.

Know Your Founding Fathers

NAME: "Mad" Anthony Wayne

BIRTHDAY: January 1, 1745

BIRTHPLACE: Easttown Township, Pennsylvania

CLAIM TO FAME: Completely fearless military commander

JOB BEFORE THE WAR: Land surveyor, tanner, politician

ROLE IN THE WAR: Commanded American troops at Brandywine, Monmouth, and Stony Point

AFTER THE WAR: Served one year as a US Representative from Georgia, then went to the Ohio Territory to command the US Army in a war against a confederacy of American Indian tribes that did not want the region to be part of the United States. He was victorious in the war and established Fort Wayne, Indiana, as a base to keep order in the region.

BONUS FACT: Wayne was great at math and was an expert land surveyor. In 1765, he went to Nova Scotia, Canada, and spent a year there drawing some of the most accurate maps of the region that had yet been produced.

The Culper Ring

The Secret World of Washington's Spies
New York City
1778–1783

> Three may keep a Secret, if two of them are dead.
>
> —Benjamin Franklin, *Poor Richard's Almanack*

W HEN THE BRITISH ARMY WRENCHED
New York City from the bloody hands of the
American military, they immediately became mas-
ters of one of the largest cities in North America. Squads
stormed the streets, and countless patriot sympathizers were
herded onto horrifying prison ships in New York Harbor,
where they were kept in miserable conditions. England sent
ship after ship of reinforcements, supplies, officers, and equipment to New York, and before long English officers in their
powdered wigs and crisp, clean uniforms were walking briskly

through every street in Manhattan. Hessian regiments took over homes and businesses as barracks. British Army sentries in full military gear stood at attention outside most government buildings. At night, fancy restaurants were packed with lords and ladies in their nicest clothing, dining by candlelight, sipping wine, or attending fancy parties.

It was the most dangerous place on earth for a patriot sympathizer (a person who supported the patriot cause), but also the best place in the world if you wanted to gain information on what the redcoats were going to do next.

Almost immediately after the Battle of Brooklyn, a Continental Army officer named Nathan Hale made an attempt to infiltrate British lines. He snuck past the guards on Long Island, surveyed the defenses, and made counts of how many soldiers and cannons they had. But right as he was about to leave, he was caught by a British sentry, who jammed a gun in Hale's face and forced him to surrender. The British didn't even give him a trial. They just handed Hale a coffin, made him carry it to the nearest tree (or so the story goes), and hanged him as a spy and a traitor. As he defiantly stood with a noose around his neck, his famous last words were *"I regret that I have but one life to give for my country."*

Nathan Hale was unquestionably brave, but he hadn't been particularly effective as a spy. If the Americans wanted to know what was happening behind enemy lines, they were going to need something a little more organized than just sending a dude to sneak around the British camp. So, in November 1778, George Washington approached his most effective reconnaissance cavalry officer, Major Benjamin Tallmadge from Setauket, Long Island. Washington commissioned Tallmadge as director of military intelligence for the Continental Army. His mission was to create a secret spy service that could get reliable, accurate information out of New York City and keep the Americans in the loop about what the heck was going on there. It would be insanely dangerous for all people involved, but the survival of America depended on it.

Tallmadge went to work immediately, contacting one of the people he knew he could trust: Abraham Woodhull, his best friend from back home in Setauket. Woodhull and Tallmadge together created what would become known as the Culper Spy Ring. It consisted of Woodhull (code name Sam Culper, Sr.), a New York City coffeehouse proprietor named Robert Townsend (code name Sam Culper, Jr.), a Long Island tavern owner named Austin Roe, a whaleboat captain named Caleb Brewster, and a farmer named Anna Smith Strong. Her husband was a patriot judge imprisoned on the prison ship HMS *Jersey* in New York Harbor.

The spy ring primarily ran through Robert Townsend's NYC coffeehouse. Townsend pretended to be a loyalist, and every time British soldiers or their wives would come into the shop Townsend would talk a bunch of trash about the patriots, ask how the war was going, and basically just try to be buddies with all the British dudes. Everyone liked him and thought he was on their side, so they'd occasionally give him some little bits of information that he could pass along to the rebels. When he wasn't working at the shop, Townsend also worked as a part-time writer for the New York loyalist newspaper, the *Royal Gazette*, which was owned by a guy named James Rivington, who may or may not have been a patriot spy as well (even now, 240 years later, we don't know for sure if Rivington was really a British loyalist or a patriot double agent! Isn't that nuts?). On the surface, Townsend was a "society reporter," which meant he got invited to fancy British officers' parties and wrote these fluffy articles about who was the best dressed or whatever. But hey, he was getting invited to parties where British officers were hanging out and drinking too much and talking about things they probably shouldn't. And Townsend would remember it all, write it down, and bring it back to the rebels. He also did a series of interviews with British officers for the *Gazette*. The Brits loved seeing their names in print, and before long guys were asking to be interviewed by him.

What's the old saying? *Keep your friends close, and your enemies closer.*

Of course, getting the information was just half the battle. Townsend also had to get it out of there without being caught. To do this, he used all kinds of cool spy tricks. First, everything was written in a special code designed by Major Tallmadge. His code book contained 763 different words, all identified by a number. So, for instance, 38 meant *attack*, 255 meant *horse*, 711 was the code for *George Washington*, and 727 was the code for *New York*. The only way to decipher the code was if you had a codebook, and the only people who had codebooks were Townsend, Woodhull, Tallmadge, and George Washington himself. For extra security, Townsend wrote these codes in a special invisible ink that would only appear if you brushed a special mixture over it.

Here's how it worked: Washington would tell Tallmadge what he wanted, and Tallmadge would send a request to tavern owner Austin Roe. Roe would write the request out in invisible ink, then ride into New York City, go to Townsend's coffeehouse, and drop off a supply order from a (fake) person named John Bolton (Tallmadge's code name). Townsend would then run the invisible-ink solution over the order, read the numbers that appeared, and figure out what info Washington needed. He'd get the info by chatting with people in his shop and going to parties. Then he'd send for Roe, saying the order was complete.

Roe would ride back to NYC and pick up his supplies (usually a big box of coffee or something). Inside the supplies was hidden another piece of paper, which Townsend had written on with invisible ink. Roe would then ride 110 miles back to Setauket and bury the letter in a secret drop box on Abraham Woodhull's farm. Woodhull would dig it up, then look across the way to Anna Strong's farm. He'd check her clothesline every day until he saw a black petticoat hanging from the line—that meant that Caleb Brewster was waiting in his boat to pick up the letter. Next to the petticoat, Strong would hang a series of handkerchiefs in a pattern that would indicate which secret cove the ship was hiding in. That night, Woodhull would sneak down to the cove and pass the letter to Brewster. Brewster would row it across the bay to Fairfield, Connecticut, and drop it off with Tallmadge. Tallmadge would reveal the message, translate it, then ride it full-speed to Washington. Sure, this might sound super-confusing and complicated, but every single step was taken to make sure the British would never figure out what the heck was going on.

For five years, from 1778 to 1783, the Culper Spy Ring ferried information out of New York City, bringing more intel to George Washington than any other group of spies in the war. Washington always knew who was coming into the city, who was going out, how much equipment they had, and where they were headed. Secrecy was of the utmost importance, though, so not even Washington knew who was involved in the ring. He only knew the spies by their code names. They were so intense with their secrets that *nobody* could confirm who Sam Culper, Jr., was until some FBI guys did handwriting analysis on the letters in the 1950s!

Of course, it didn't always go smoothly. In July 1779, Tallmadge was attacked by a British cavalry unit under the command of Banastre Tarleton (you'll hear more about him in chapter 19). Tarleton's Raiders shot Tallmadge's horse out from under him, and although Tallmadge was able to escape, some of his letters were captured. The British couldn't figure out the code, but they were able to trace one of the letters back to a New York City man named George Higday, whom the Culpers were thinking about bringing into the ring. Higday luckily received word that the papers were stolen, and he had time to destroy all the evidence before the British raided his house and tore it apart looking for info. British troops also went to Abraham Woodhull's house and beat up his dad trying to get info, but the Woodhulls didn't give up anything. Throughout the entire war, not a single Culper Ring spy was captured by the British.

Their information was extremely effective as well. At one point, the Culpers were able to steal the British naval codebook from a Royal Navy officer. Another time (two times, actually!), they got the help of a local tailor named Hercules Mulligan and uncovered a plot to assassinate George Washington! Yet another time, they discovered that General Henry Clinton was sending the entire British Army to ambush the French Army as soon as it landed at Newport, Rhode Island. This info was so important that Austin Roe broke protocol, wrote the note in invisible ink between the lines of a letter he'd stolen from a well-known loyalist, and rode it straight through enemy lines (bluffing his way past a couple of British checkpoints in the process). He didn't stop until he handed it personally to Washington's aide, Alexander Hamilton.

The Culpers also played a role in the discovery of the biggest spy plot in the American Revolution, a British plan to sabotage the American fortress at West Point, New York. To its shock and horror, the Culper Spy Ring intercepted a letter from Clinton's spymaster, Major John André, indicating that he was in secret contact with one of the rebels' greatest war heroes and that the two men were working together to betray the patriots.

John André was going to meet with American general Benedict Arnold, the hero of Fort Ticonderoga, Quebec City, and Saratoga, to discuss the possibility of surrendering West Point to the British!

In the years since Saratoga, Benedict Arnold had been seething. Recovering from his wounds, he had been put in charge of Philadelphia, where he married into a loyalist family and was accused by the Continental Congress of stealing government funds for his personal use. His leg hurt every day. He was passed over for promotion. And now he'd been placed in command of the fort at West Point, and he was really angry. He met with John André on September 20, 1780, and agreed to surrender the fort to the British in exchange for a ton of money and an officer's commission in the British Army.

A group of New York militiamen captured John André on his way back from the meeting with Arnold. In his boot, they found letters from Arnold confirming the worst.

Washington was livid. He stormed to West Point to confront Arnold. When he got there, he saw that Arnold had refused Washington's orders to fortify the base and was gone, slipped away aboard a British ship...the HMS *Vulture* from the last chapter. Washington tried to make a deal with General Clinton: "We will trade you André for Arnold." But Clinton refused, so Washington had André hanged as a spy.

The discovery of Arnold's treason rocked America to its core. Nobody could believe it. To this day, the name Benedict Arnold is a synonym for *traitor*, which is a sad ending for a once-heroic soldier.

But still, the discovery of Arnold's treason and the hundreds of other discoveries of the Culper Spy Ring helped save

America from what could have been a completely devastating blow. These six men and women—Tallmadge, Woodhull, Townsend, Roe, Brewster, and Strong—might not have had all the glory of great military heroes kicking butt on the battlefield. But they risked constant life-threatening danger to provide some of the most important intelligence of the war, and their actions saved thousands of lives—and possibly even the Revolution.

AGENT 355

When you read about the Culper Spy Ring, there's occasionally a bunch of talk about "Agent 355," a high-society noblewoman who may have been a friend of John André. According to the story, Agent 355 got a lot of information about André's plans but was eventually arrested and died aboard the prison ship HMS *Jersey*. Well, this probably isn't true. In Tallmadge's codebook, *355* was simply code for *the lady*, and women were not kept on the prison ships. Since Anna Strong was a known member of the Culper Ring, and she was often permitted to visit her husband aboard HMS *Jersey*, one likely theory is that "Agent 355" is actually just Anna Strong. Strong, by the way, survived the war and collected a pension for her service to the American military.

CAN'T TRUST THOSE SCHOOLTEACHERS

The patriots weren't the only ones who used spies in the war. The British employed a woman named Ann Bates, a Philadelphia schoolteacher, to help them gather info on the Americans. Posing as a merchant, Bates would enter the American camps and act like she was selling food, sewing kits to repair uniforms, games, and playing cards. While she was in the camp, she'd make mental counts of artillery pieces, gun calibers, and troop dispositions. She made dozens of trips behind enemy lines, sometimes hiding in cellars, evading rebel patrols, or escorting other spies to their objectives. Another highly effective loyalist spy was a woman known only as Miss Jenny, a French-speaking loyalist who reported on enemy positions and was so good at it that we still don't know her real name to this day!

"A FLOATING HELL"

When the British ran out of room in their jails, they started loading patriot prisoners into old ships docked off the shores of Brooklyn and just leaving them there to rot. These prison ships were overcrowded, and disease, malnutrition, and death happened daily. Men were given very little food or water, had no beds to sleep on, and were kept in almost complete darkness in the holds of the ships. When prisoners would die, usually of smallpox, typhoid, dysentery, yellow fever, heat exhaustion, or starvation, their bodies would just be thrown overboard. The most notorious of these ships was the HMS *Jersey*, which housed about a thousand prisoners. But there were eleven prison ships in total. While we still don't know for sure, many historians believe that an incredible eleven thousand people died aboard prison ships during the war—way more than were actually killed by gunfire or bayonets during the Revolution.

The Treason of Benedict Arnold

After Arnold's treason was discovered, he became a brigadier general in the British Army. He participated in the burning of rebel supplies in Richmond, Virginia, and even burned down his hometown, New London, Connecticut, setting fire to the houses of his former neighbors and friends. After the war, he returned to England and became a businessman, but he was never super-successful.

There are three monuments to Benedict Arnold in the United States. Two of them are on the battlefield at Saratoga. One, a statue of a boot, is placed at the spot where Arnold led the charge that won the battle. It

simply says, IN MEMORY OF THE MOST BRILLIANT SOLDIER OF
THE CONTINENTAL ARMY, WHO WAS DESPERATELY WOUNDED ON
THIS SPOT...WINNING FOR HIS COUNTRYMEN THE DECISIVE BAT-
TLE OF THE AMERICAN REVOLUTION, AND FOR HIMSELF THE RANK
OF MAJOR GENERAL. Elsewhere on the battlefield, a large
statue depicts all the American commanders at Saratoga.
Three of the niches on the monument feature larger-
than-life statues of Horatio Gates, Philip Schuyler, and
Daniel Morgan. The fourth is empty.

Statue of Benedict Arnold's boot

On the grounds of the United States Military Academy,
which is where the fortress at West Point once stood,
there is a hall where plaques depict every American general of the Revolution. The plaques list the birth year,

rank, death year, and a little sentence or two of detail. As you walk down this long line of plaques, there is one that simply reads MAJOR GENERAL, BORN 1740. There are no additional details.

During Arnold's raid into Virginia in 1781, the general decided to personally interrogate one of the American soldiers he had taken prisoner. The prisoner didn't realize he was talking to Arnold, so Arnold asked if there were any orders regarding what to do if the patriots captured the great traitor Benedict Arnold. The soldier is said to have replied, "Yes, we are to bury the wounded leg with the highest military honors...and hang the rest of him."

According to legend, while he was on his deathbed, Arnold asked his son to retrieve his old Continental Army uniform. The story claims that his last words were "Let me die in this old uniform in which I fought my battles. May God forgive me for ever having put on another."

Know Your Founding Fathers

NAME: Benjamin Tallmadge

BIRTHDAY: February 25, 1754

BIRTHPLACE: Setauket, New York

CLAIM TO FAME: Head of the Culper Spy Ring

JOB BEFORE THE WAR: Superintendent of Wethersfield
   High School in Wethersfield, Connecticut

ROLE IN THE WAR: Gathered intelligence on British
   operations in New York City

AFTER THE WAR: Postmaster for the town of Litchfield,
   Connecticut; served in Congress for sixteen years

BONUS FACT: His son Frederick was the New York City
   Police Commissioner from 1857 to 1862.

The War on the Frontier

George Rogers Clark Captures Six Future US States

The Northwest Territories
June 16, 1778—February 6, 1779

> Great things have been affected by
> a few men well conducted.
>
> —Major George Rogers Clark, Virginia Militia

W E LOVE TO CELEBRATE THANKSGIVING with fun school plays, giant hocks of turkey leg, and coloring book pages of Pilgrims and American Indians shaking hands and hugging in front of a big rainbow while singing songs from Disney's *Pocahontas*. But a huge part of the history of America is the story of European settlers locked in bloody, vicious, horrific warfare with the native inhabitants of the land. Heck, even when the Vikings landed in Canada in AD 1001, *they* ended up fighting the American Indians (for more on this, check out *Guts & Glory: The Vikings*).

The never-ending struggle between settlers and American Indians is one of the most horrific and longest-lasting battles in human history. Basically (and this is a massive overgeneralization), European people landed in North America, and since there were no other white people here, they decided the land was theirs. So they built houses, farmed, killed wild animals, hunted for furs, and did all the things a colonist would need to do to stay alive and make money in the wilderness. Well, the American Indians already lived here, and they didn't like these settlers taking over like they owned the place. So for the next couple hundred years there were guys killing each other, burning down houses, stealing each other's stuff, and doing all sorts of other terrible things that people really shouldn't do to each other.

Well, the sad truth is that there were plenty of people out there willing to take advantage of this destruction. And in the early years of the Revolution, a particularly nasty British colonel named Henry Hamilton was one of them. Colonel Hamilton was the commander of the fort at Detroit, and his nickname was the "Hair Buyer," because he would pay money to any American Indian warrior who took the scalp from a dead Colonial settler. Native warriors, eager to collect the bounty, started brutally raiding Colonial settlements, killing men, women, and children, burning down villages, and then trading the scalps to Hamilton for British cash, furs, ammunition, weapons, food, and equipment.

This had to stop. And one man decided he was the guy to do it. Even better, he decided he was going to accomplish this mission without killing anyone.

George Rogers Clark was born November 19, 1752, on a small farm outside Charlottesville, Virginia. A big, strong, red-headed country boy, Clark learned land surveying and map-making from his grandfather. As soon as he was old enough, he traveled through Boone's Pass to Kentucky to try to explore some new lands that colonists hadn't visited before. He climbed mountains, passed through forests, fought off bears, and forded rivers on homemade rafts, mapping out land and finding good spots for crops, hunting, and towns. Once he was done with that, he led other colonists out there to set up villages on the land that today is part of the state of Kentucky.

When all these reports of destruction and horror started coming in, Clark went to Virginia to ask for help from Thomas Jefferson and Governor Patrick Henry. After a bit of persuasion, Henry commissioned Clark as a major in the Virginia Militia and gave him permission to raise soldiers to fight the Hair Buyer.

George Rogers Clark recruited a group of about 150 men and set out to try to attack the British holdings in the Northwest Territory (a humongous section of wilderness up by the Great Lakes). Crossing the Ohio River, this group of settlers and mountain men landed in a thick forest where they hunted and lived off the land as they marched north to Kaskaskia, a small British fort in present-day Illinois. Kaskaskia was defended by only a few redcoats, and those guys ran away as soon as Clark's men showed up. Clark captured the town for America without firing a single bullet.

Now, an interesting thing about the frontier territory there is that this entire center part of the current United States used to be owned by France. So the hundred or so people who lived in Kaskaskia were pretty much all French. The French hated the British, sure, but they also weren't fond of the Americans (who hadn't been cool with the fact that most French people were Catholic). But George Rogers Clark didn't care about that. He wasn't going to burn down Catholic churches or force everyone to become Baptist or something. He got the people together, kindly told them they could go about their normal lives, and asked if any of them wanted to help him fight the British.

The French joined up immediately. Even better, a French priest named Père Gibault traveled over to the town of Vincennes (in present-day Indiana) and persuaded them to join America, too.

Clark's next order of business was to deal with the native tribes in the area. But once again, instead of fighting, he called the chiefs of all the local tribes together to talk about peace. He was kind and diplomatic and offered the native tribes a truce. Many of them agreed to forbid their warriors to take Colonel Henry Hamilton up on his horrible offer to pay for scalps. After that, Clark established trade along the Mississippi with the Spanish-controlled city of New Orleans, bringing up supplies, food, weapons, and other goods.

Just like that, without firing a shot, George Rogers Clark almost single-handedly drove the British out of two frontier towns, captured a humongous amount of land for America, made peace with the American Indians, made peace with the French, and established trade with the Spanish.

Back in Detroit, Hair Buyer Hamilton was so mad that his face was the same color as his red officer's jacket. He gathered his troops, loaded them into canoes, and headed out on a grueling journey with five hundred men to smash Clark and his little band of militiamen into traitor stew. A few weeks later, a screaming group of redcoats, American Indian warriors, and French militia conscripts came charging out of the woods and stormed Vincennes, which surrendered without a fight.

Clark was nearly two hundred miles away in the town of Kaskaskia when this went down. He had only 172 soldiers with him, and it was the beginning of winter. But he knew he couldn't back down now that his target was finally in sight. He ordered his men to follow him, and in February 1779, George Rogers Clark went on an insane overland journey that rivaled

Benedict Arnold's journey to Canada in chapter 5. Traveling
for seventeen days through 180 miles of rain, snow, flooding,
ice, and forest, this motley group of pioneers braved incredible dangers. Cougars, grizzly bears, waterfalls, rapids, and
floodplains stood in their path. During the day they walked
or canoed through shoulder-deep ice water in the dead of the
Illinois winter. At night they slept in trees to stay dry. Men
got sick from the cold, or caught the flu, and the water was so
deep at one point that the drummer boy had to ride his drum
like an inner tube to avoid drowning.

After over two weeks of this misery, the Americans reached
the outskirts of Vincennes. The town was at the bottom
of a hill, and Hamilton's British were in a fort at the top
of the hill. Hamilton outnumbered Clark, and his fort was
really impressive, with eleven-foot-high wooden walls,
towers with cannons on them,
and a big ditch out
front with a gate like
in an old castle.

Clark's men camped
just outside town.
They built fires, dried
out their clothes,
cooked the last of their
food, and prepared for
an epic showdown.

Then, suddenly, one of the French settlers of Vincennes came up to the camp to see what was going on. Clark met him and gave him a bold statement: "Tell the people of Vincennes that the Americans are going to capture the town tomorrow. If you are with us, then stay in your homes and don't come outside. If you are with the British, go to the fort now."

The settler ran back with the news. Not a single Vincennes settler went to the fort.

The next day, once again without a shot, George Rogers Clark marched into Vincennes. The drummer played, and Clark had his men walk around the town all day long so the redcoats watching from the fort thought there were a *lot* more Americans than there actually were. Meanwhile, in the town, the people of Vincennes ran outside and offered the Americans food, ammunition, and clean clothes.

Now it was time to deal with the fort—and Hair Buyer Hamilton.

George Rogers Clark knew he didn't have enough men to take the fort with an assault, so he fought the way he would have hunted deer in the wilderness. He had his men hide in the forest and use their long rifles to accurately shoot any redcoats they saw on the walls of the fort. After having a few of their guys sniped, the redcoats fired their cannons, but they couldn't really see the Americans to hit them. After a couple of days of this, realizing he was now surrounded by snipers, with no idea how many men Clark had, and without

any reinforcements coming, Colonel Hamilton surrendered the fort. He came outside and offered his sword to Clark, and the Virginia militiaman sent the Hair Buyer back to Richmond with nearly six hundred British prisoners of war. He was shocked when he realized Clark had only 150 guys with him.

American Indian raids on settlements decreased almost immediately.

Clark was promoted to brigadier general for his heroic capture of the Northwest Territories, and he spent the rest of the war stationed around present-day Louisville, Kentucky. He

Postage stamp commemorating George Rogers Clark's victory at Vincennes

faced a few more American Indian attacks, but nothing like before. He tried to make plans to attack and capture Detroit, but the Continental Congress never sent him enough soldiers to attempt it.

Okay, so this story didn't involve epic heroic attacks, charges, hand-to-hand combat, and cavalry raids, but consider this for a minute: With just 150 men and only a few gunshots, George Rogers Clark captured from the British the territories that would eventually become the states of Kentucky, Missouri, Illinois, Ohio, Michigan, and Indiana. This man, acting by himself and with no support, gained a chunk of land that would almost *double the size of the Colonial United States* once the peace treaty was signed.

HIS KID BROTHER WAS OKAY, TOO

In the early 1800s, George Rogers Clark's little brother William Clark set out with his best friend, Meriwether Lewis, on an epic two-year journey to explore and map vast areas of uncharted North American land. Financed by President Thomas Jefferson in 1804, the Lewis and Clark Expedition traveled from Saint Louis all the way to the Pacific Ocean near present-day Portland, Oregon. Aided by their American Indian guide, Sacajawea, and her knowledge of the land, Lewis and Clark discovered mountains, waterfalls, and rivers. They canoed, hiked, drew maps, made treaties with the native tribes, and studied previously unknown wildlife and minerals of the Great Plains, Columbia River Basin, and Pacific Northwest. Their contributions would lead to dozens of amazing scientific discoveries and would pave the way for Americans to settle the western half of North America.

Know Your Founding Fathers

NAME: George Rogers Clark

BIRTHDAY: November 19, 1752

BIRTHPLACE: Charlottesville, Virginia

CLAIM TO FAME: Opened up the Northwest for American settlement

JOB BEFORE THE WAR: Land surveyor, militia leader

ROLE IN THE WAR: Commander of American forces in the Northwest Territories

AFTER THE WAR: Clark retired to a small plot of land and eventually fell into poverty. He almost helped France attack the Spanish forces in New Orleans, but that plan never came to fruition.

BONUS FACT: Clark was commissioned to survey a project that would build a canal around the Falls of the Ohio River, but that plan failed when one of the members of the board of directors for the project—Vice President Aaron Burr—was arrested for treason for secretly plotting to overthrow the American government.

Not Yet Begun to Fight

John Paul Jones vs. HMS *Serapis*
Flamborough Head, England
September 23, 1779

> I wish to have no connection with any ship that does not sail fast; for I intend to go in harm's way.
>
> —Captain John Paul Jones, United States Navy

FROM THE BEGINNING OF THE WAR IT WAS pretty dang clear to everyone in the world that the Continental Navy had absolutely zero chance of taking on Great Britain on the high seas. England's navy was too strong, and any kind of drawn-out naval warfare would leave the Americans bombarded into toothpicks. The British Royal Navy had hundreds of warships crewed by experienced sailors, highly trained officers, and master gunners, and they dominated the high seas. Nobody in their right mind would have tried to take them on in a battle....

Unless, of course, you were Captain John Paul Jones, the Father of the US Navy. For this daring naval commander, nothing was too crazy—not even ramming a forty-gun British battleship while his own vessel was sinking and on fire and half his crew was dead.

But let's back up. When the war started in 1775, Congress was desperate for any men or ships it could find to help with the war effort. America had no military vessels at all, and even if it did, taking on an eighteenth-century British warship gun-to-gun was a suicide mission. Despite the odds, Congress still put out a call to hire sailors and gunboats to smuggle goods past the British blockade, attack lightly armed British resupply transport ships, or do anything they could possibly think of to disrupt enemy operations.

John Paul Jones was one of the first men to respond to the call. Born in Scotland, Jones had spent most of his life working aboard slave ships and other trading vessels that ran from Charleston, South Carolina, to the Caribbean, to England. Jones was a very successful and knowledgeable sailor, having captained a number of ships, but he was also a hotheaded party monster who used lots of bad language and had an even worse temper. Once, a member of his crew refused to follow orders, so John Paul Jones had the guy tied to the mast and flogged with a whip so hard that the guy eventually died.

Another time, in 1773, his crew organized a mutiny, so Jones had their leader executed.

Accused of murder for taking out the mutiny's leader, Jones fled the Caribbean to his brother's farm in Fredericksburg, Virginia, to lie low for a while. But once times got tough for the colonies, the American navy was willing to overlook something like "accidentally killing a guy and then killing another guy on purpose" as long as the dude doing the killing knew how to handle a ship. The navy was that hard up for anybody who knew what the heck a mizzenmast was (so, yeah, look that nautical term up, because it might just get you a job someday).

Jones volunteered to join the fledgling Continental Navy and was given the prestigious title of senior first lieutenant aboard one of the few warships the American navy was able to put together. He was the first man to hoist a United States naval ensign (flag) over a US vessel, and he served as second-in-command on the thirty-gun ship *Alfred*. Basically, later in life John Paul Jones would be Captain Picard, but he got his start as Commander Riker. The *Alfred* spent the first months of the war sailing up and down the East Coast of America sacking and plundering British merchant vessels as they tried to deliver supplies to the redcoats.

Here's a fun fact: As first mate on the *Alfred*, John Paul Jones participated in the first military action ever undertaken by the United States Marine Corps. On the night of March 3, 1776, the Continental Navy attacked the capital of the Bahamas in a daring night raid, unloading 234 marines onto the island. Dressed in green Continental Army jackets and led by their first commandant, Samuel Nichols, the marines stormed the fort of Nassau, overran the garrison, and captured 88 cannons, 15 mortars, 24 barrels of gunpowder, and, awesomely, the governor of the Bahamas. Then they ran a "Don't Tread on Me" flag up from the fort and took off with their plunder.

Having proved himself worth his sea salts, Jones was given command of the twelve-gun sloop *Providence* and was sent out by Congress to wreak havoc on anything flying a Union Jack. Jones did this quite well, capturing sixteen British vessels in six weeks. On November 2, 1776, he assaulted the British Coal Fleet at Isle Royale (which is in the middle of Lake Superior!), destroying a large portion of the merchant ships, liberating a handful of American prisoners of war who were being held on the island, and capturing a British vessel full of cozy winter clothing intended for the British troops stationed in Canada and New York.

On the heels of his success as captain of the *Providence*, Jones was given command of the eighteen-gun frigate *Ranger* and sent to France to help the US cause there. He headed for Paris, spent his nights partying with his buddy Benjamin Franklin, and lived the good life while the French decided whether they were going to ally with America and join the war.

Once France officially entered the war on the side of the Americans, Jones immediately took the crew of the *Ranger* to England. As he departed France, the *Ranger* received a formal military salute from the French fleet, marking the first time a US vessel had ever been officially saluted by a foreign warship. He then assaulted the British town of Whitehaven in the middle of the night in a daring raid during which he and sixteen other dudes set fire to the fleet that was stationed there.

Following this, he raided the private estate of the Earl of Selkirk, a gigantic mansion on prime beachfront property on the English coast. Jones had hoped to capture the earl and ransom him in exchange for US sailors who had been forced into British service. But when JPJ and his minions arrived at the estate, they found that the earl was out of town on a business trip or something. So Jones and his guys had a nice cup of afternoon tea with the earl's wife before stealing a set of silver dishes and reboarding the *Ranger*. Jones would later return most of these dishes to the countess with a letter of apology, because it's really just bad form to rip off someone who invited you in for tea and conversation. Either way, when news hit the American papers that a Continental Navy warship was stealing dishes from an English earl's house, patriots everywhere were high-fiving and clinking their juice glasses together in triumph.

On the way back to France to resupply, Jones came across

the twenty-gun British sloop of war HMS *Drake*, a legitimate warship unlike the shipping vessels Jones had taken on before. Jones knew that no American had ever successfully traded shots with a real British warship, but where most people would have gotten scared, he saw an opportunity to do something awesome. He ordered his crew to raise battle sails, run out the guns, and close to firing range.

The two warships engaged, and in a fierce one-hour battle the *Ranger* defeated the *Drake*, killing forty men (including the captain) and capturing the vessel. News of this victory further boosted American spirits, as it was the first successful battle fought by American forces in English waters, and it was the Continental Navy's first military victory over a British warship.

Jones returned to Paris and ended up spending a few days talking strategy with the Marquis de Lafayette. Once the two men figured out a plan of attack, Jones was officially given command of the massively impressive USS *Bonhomme Richard*, a large French trading vessel that had been refitted as a towering forty-two-gun frigate. It was by far the biggest and baddest ship in the US fleet, and Jones was about to take it into an epic fight that would make him a legend.

On September 23, 1779, the *Bonhomme Richard* came across a fleet of around forty British trading ships being escorted by the forty-four-gun frigate *Serapis* and the twenty-eight-gun *Countess of Scarborough*. Jones ordered his squadron of US and French Navy ships to attack, and his *Bonhomme Richard* hurtled toward *Serapis* for an old-school, life-or-death, face-smashing brawl. Devastating broadsides (when all the guns on the side of a ship fire at the same time) from *Serapis* blew apart the *Bonhomme Richard*'s sides, knocking out several of her main-deck cannons and crippling the ship. Jones fired back with ripping cannon broadsides of his own, but relentless volleys from the larger and more heavily armed *Serapis* raked Jones's ship with explosive shrapnel and fire.

Jones was forced to abandon all his lower-deck guns as the *Bonhomme Richard* continued heroically firing its remaining cannons. But the *Serapis* swung around, sighted its guns, and unleashed a crushing barrage of cannon fire that smashed the mast of the *Bonhomme Richard* and blasted apart the deck. Captain Richard Pearson of the *Serapis* called across to the Americans to ask for their surrender. Jones took a look at the burning wreckage of his crippled warship, which was taking on water, burning with black smoke, and littered with dead bodies, set his jaw, and declared:

"Surrender? I have not yet begun to fight!"

Jones then spun the pilot's wheel, pointed the *Bonhomme Richard* straight at the British ship, and rammed the *Serapis*, wrapping the two ships together and intertwining their rigging. The *Serapis* attempted to pull away from the *Bonhomme Richard* so it could use its cannons on the almost-defenseless American ship, but Jones's sailors threw grappling hooks over the side, pulled hard, and lashed the two ships closer together.

More of Jones's desperate men ran to the side of the ship with muskets and threw homemade bombs at the *Serapis*'s deck, setting fire to the British ship and killing several Royal Navy sailors. A large group of British marines rushed forward in an attempt to board the American vessel, but Jones organized his troops to fire a volley that drove them back. Then, sword held high, John Paul Jones personally led a group of his own men over to the *Serapis*. Fighting with swords, pistols, and muskets, Jones and the Americans overcame the British, and Captain Pearson surrendered the flag.

By the time the sun set that evening, both ships were crippled, had lost over half of their men, and were on fire in numerous places. The *Bonhomme Richard* had to be abandoned the following morning when attempts to bail several feet of water out of its hold didn't work. It sank to the bottom of the North Sea, but John Paul Jones took his entire crew over to the *Serapis* and sailed away as the new captain.

For his success in this heated battle against a British warship, John Paul Jones was knighted by King Louis XVI of France and given a gold-plated ceremonial sword to replace the one he'd just busted up in battle. Jones also received the Order of Military Merit from the French government and was issued a Congressional Gold Medal by the United States Continental Congress in 1787. The Brits still thought of him as little better than a criminal and demanded that he be hanged as a pirate.

> An honorable Peace is and always was my first wish! I can take no delight in the effusion of human Blood; but, if this War should continue, I wish to have the most active part in it.
>
> —John Paul Jones

STILL FIGHTING, EVEN AFTER THE WAR

After the Revolution, JPJ headed over to Russia, called himself
Pavel Dzhones, and went into the service of Empress Catherine
the Great. Jones was made a rear admiral and given command
of the Imperial Navy's twenty-four-gun flagship *Vladimir*. He led
the Russian defense of the Black Sea against the Ottoman Turks
and was awarded the Order of Saint Anne. He retired to Paris,
where he died in 1792. His remains were returned to the United
States and were placed in the United States Naval Academy chapel
in Annapolis, Maryland, in an awesome sarcophagus modeled
after Napoleon's coffin.

SEMPER FI

On November 10, 1775, the Second Continental Congress created
two battalions of American marines to help fight in the war. The
marines' first commanding officer, Samuel Nichols, headed to
the Tun Tavern and brewery in Philadelphia. There he recruited
a group of leathernecks eager to take the battle to the British.
Dressed in green jackets and fighting aboard Continental Navy
vessels, the marines participated in raids and naval battles
throughout the war. To this day, the Marine Corps celebrates its
birthday on November 10.

Know Your Founding Fathers

NAME: John Paul Jones

BIRTHDAY: July 6, 1747

BIRTHPLACE: Arbigland, Scotland

CLAIM TO FAME: Father of the United States Navy

JOB BEFORE THE WAR: Merchant ship officer

ROLE IN THE WAR: Commanding officer, USS *Ranger* and USS *Bonhomme Richard*

AFTER THE WAR: Rear admiral in the Russian Navy from 1783 to 1789

BONUS FACT: Jones's body is entombed in a marble-and-bronze sarcophagus at the United States Naval Academy. An honor guard stands at attention next to the sarcophagus whenever his crypt is open to the public.

Deborah Sampson

The Adventures of Private Robert Shurtleff

Massachusetts and New York
1780–1782

> **God helps those that help themselves.**
>
> —Benjamin Franklin, *Poor Richard's Almanack*

RATHER THAN FOCUSING ON A SPECIFIC battle, campaign, or mission, this chapter is the story of Continental Army Private Robert Shurtleff of the Fourth Massachusetts Infantry Regiment. Shurtleff was a front-line skirmish ranger who survived multiple life-threatening situations. He shouldered a musket in face-to-face battles against redcoats all across upstate New York during the closing days of the Revolution. Once, he survived being sliced in the head with a cavalry saber. But Robert Shurtleff isn't just notable because he was a tough sucker who put his life on the line in deadly circumstances, fought with the ferociousness of a pinned-down wolverine, and took two bullets for his country.

He is notable because he was actually a woman named Deborah Sampson, who tricked everyone into thinking she was a guy and fought throughout the war with the Continental Army.

Deborah Sampson was born in Plympton, Massachusetts, on December 17, 1760, into a family that was about as American as a bald eagle wolfing down hamburger patties at an NFL tailgate party. Her great-great-etc.-grandparents John and Priscilla Alden were original gangsta Pilgrims who landed on Plymouth Rock, but at some point down the road her dad lost a ton of money on bad investments and ditched his family, never to be heard from again. (Some people think he was killed in a shipwreck, while others claim he moved to Maine and started a new family.) Deborah was just five years old when this went down, but her mom still split her up from her brothers and sisters and shipped her off to live with some random family friends in Massachusetts. She bounced from house to house for five years; then, at the ripe old age of ten, she was sold by one of her foster families into indentured servitude, where she basically worked as a slave on some plantation out in Middleborough. For the next eight years. Welcome to the real world, kid.

As an indentured servant, Deborah wasn't allowed to go to school or get an education. But as this tall, powerfully built, determined teenage girl grew strong from long, hard days working in the field, she also taught herself to read and write. Plowing by day and reading political pamphlets by night, Sampson somehow managed to educate herself to the point where she got a job as a schoolteacher pretty much immediately after she was released from her servitude (on her eighteenth birthday!).

Well, the life of a 1780s schoolmarm didn't end up being all that appealing to Deborah Sampson. First, she had an obnoxious encounter with some goofball who'd fallen in love with her (she is said to have described him as having "all the *sang-froid* of a Frenchman and the silliness of a baboon"). Deborah "set him down a fool or in a fair way to be one," which makes absolutely no sense to me but I bet it's some super-clever old-school trash-talking, and then she decided, "Yeah, forget this, I'm outta here." At the time, it was literally illegal for women not to wear big pretty dresses all the time, so Deborah Sampson used her income to buy a bunch of cloth, secretly stitched herself a pair of pants, dressed up as a man, and went off to enlist in the Continental Army in 1781.

Sampson failed on her first attempt to become a soldier when someone in the army recruiting office recognized her by the weird way she held a pen (she'd had one of her fingers seriously jacked up in an encounter with a robber that I wish I knew more about). The recruiting sergeant told her he'd have her arrested if she attempted to enlist again. So she walked out the front door and several miles up the road to the next town, and three months later she enlisted with the crew of a privateer warship that was headed off to sink British supply ships off Cape Cod.

   Deborah Sampson's pirate career lasted about two days. It turned out the captain she signed on with was a raging maniac who enjoyed screaming at and beating up his sailors, so she jumped ship, headed to Uxbridge, and enlisted in the Continental Army under the fake name Robert Shurtleff. When the uniform they issued her didn't fit, she didn't mess around worrying that the company tailor might notice she wasn't a guy—she grabbed a needle and thread and altered the uniform herself.

   Private Shurtleff mustered in (joined up) with the Fourth Massachusetts Infantry Regiment and was sent to West Point, New

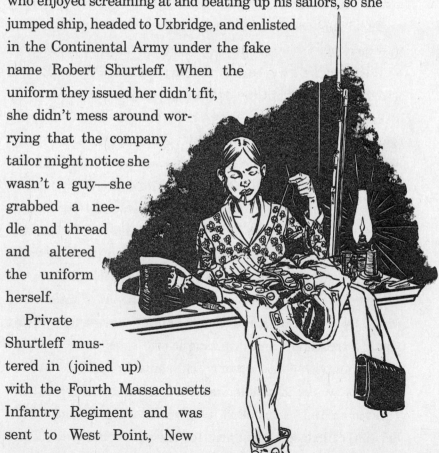

York, to do battle with the British infantry that was still occupying New York City. Standing about five foot seven and more than tough enough to handle the brutal drilling of the Continental Army, Sampson fit right in with the other troops. Apparently, she was so convincing as an ultra-manly warrior that the other troops didn't even flinch. They did, however, jokingly make fun of her because she never had to shave (they assumed this was because she was just a teenage boy), and they gave her a hilariously appropriate nickname: Molly.

During her three years of military service, Private Robert Shurtleff was on frontline duty for roughly seventeen months of combat. Part of the Fourth Infantry's Light Infantry Company (a unit of scouts and lightly equipped rangers), Shurtleff saw her first action in a hardcore battle against loyalist forces outside White Plains, New York. Charging head-on into battle, bayonet at the ready, she stormed the enemy trench and continued to fight in brutal hand-to-hand combat despite receiving a sword wound to the head from a loyalist saber. For most people, you'd think getting whacked in the dome with a sword would at least put them out of action for a while. But Sampson made a career out of constantly refusing medical treatment and "walking it off" every time someone drilled her with a fist, bayonet, rifle butt, or bullet.

A few weeks later she was shot in the shoulder outside Tarrytown and just sucked it up and walked around with a Brit bullet lodged in her arm for the rest of her life. Think about that the next time someone tells you whining is for girls.

Four months after being shot in the shoulder, Deborah Sampson was out with a small company of thirty other soldiers. Their plan was to attack a loyalist camp, set it on fire, and steal all the horses. The mission went off just as planned, but as she was chasing down a fleeing loyalist (while riding on the horse she had just stolen from him, which is pretty hilarious), some guy popped up and planted a .69-caliber chunk of hot lead right in her upper thigh. She finished off the loyalist she had been chasing but then slumped from her horse, covered in blood. One of her comrades rode her six miles to the hospital, Deborah barely hanging on to consciousness. But Deborah Sampson would rather have died in battle than go back to her old life. So instead of being seen by the surgeon, she went into the surrounding woods and dug the bullet out of her leg with a pocketknife.

It took her three tries to get it out. With a three-inch pocketknife blade. And no anesthesia.

Sampson refused further medical treatment, strapped a tourniquet on her leg, and walked out of the hospital. Two weeks later one of her squad mates came down with malaria, so she volunteered to stay behind the main body of the unit and take care of him, a move that also bought her time to heal. Unfortunately, they were resting in the home of a guy who claimed to be a patriot but was actually a loyalist sympathizer, and he gave such poor medical care to the sick soldier

that the dude died. Then the guy locked Deborah in his attic and told her he was going to hold her prisoner until the British Army came and arrested her. Naturally, she escaped (with the help of a girl who was crushing hard on Private Shurtleff), found a crew of local militia, and had the guy and fourteen other Tories arrested there.

The adventures of Private Robert Shurtleff continued well into 1782, long after the Battle of Yorktown. In 1782, she took a raiding party to the headwaters of the Hudson to fight American Indians, receiving a written commendation for bravery in the face of the enemy. A few months after that, she was part of a unit that was ambushed by loyalist forces, and she had to jump into the freezing river and swim across it in the dead of winter while enemy troops shot at her. She nearly drowned, but her quick thinking helped save the lives of many men in her company who followed her.

In the summer of 1783, Sampson was appointed aide-de-camp (assistant) to a General Patterson, but when she fell sick and was hospitalized, the army doctor was pretty surprised to realize that Private Robert Shurtleff wasn't who "he" said he was. The doctor nursed Sampson back to health, then sent her back to her commander with a letter explaining the situation. Unfortunately, her ship was caught in a storm and sunk. According to the stories, Sampson nearly drowned but somehow managed to escape the wreckage and swim to shore.

Sampson gave the letter to her commander and confessed that she wasn't actually a dude. Pretty much everyone was like, "Holy crap," but since she'd been a loyal soldier for three long years of the war, they didn't freak out the way you might expect. General Henry Knox gave her an honorable discharge from the military, allowing her to keep her uniform and collect a war veteran's pension...making her another of the very few women to receive that honor from the Continental military.

After the war, Deborah Sampson got married, had three kids, and bought a farm. She became pretty legendary after writing her memoirs and traveling the country as a public

Deborah Sampson, engraved by George Graham, from a drawing by William Beastall, based on a painting by Joseph Stone

speaker, and she lived to be sixty-eight years old. She would be the first woman officially recognized as serving in the US Army.

She certainly wouldn't be the last.

IT'S A START

In the years before the American Revolution, it was basically impossible to free a slave. Even if you owned the slave and wanted to set him or her free, you needed special permission from your state government, and this was basically never granted. All that changed with Virginia's Manumission Act of 1782, which allowed slaveholders to grant freedom to any African-Americans who had served in the Revolutionary War (there are only eight documented cases of this actually happening, unfortunately). The Manumission Act also made it legal for a slave owner to set his slaves free—Thomas Jefferson freed three of his slaves immediately after the war ended. George Washington and Benjamin Franklin freed their slaves in their wills. Also, around this time several Northern states, including Massachusetts and Pennsylvania, abolished slavery outright, and by 1810 it is estimated that roughly 14 percent of the black people in America were free. Not a great number, for sure, but it was a start.

Know Your Founding Fathers

NAME: Deborah Sampson Gannett

BIRTHDAY: December 17, 1760

BIRTHPLACE: Plympton, Massachusetts

CLAIM TO FAME: One of the only known women soldiers in the American Revolution

JOB BEFORE THE WAR: Teacher and weaver

ROLE IN THE WAR: Served in the Fourth Massachusetts Infantry Regiment under the name Robert Shurtleff

AFTER THE WAR: Honorably discharged in 1783 and married farmer Benjamin Gannett in 1785. They had four children (one adopted), and she would occasionally travel the States giving talks about her experiences in the war.

BONUS FACT: She had six brothers and sisters and is believed to have been five feet seven inches tall at a time when most women were only around five feet tall.

Butcher Tarleton

Bloody Banastre and the War in the South

South Carolina and North Carolina
March 29, 1780–March 15, 1781

> *Afterwards, in England, he had the effrontery to boast, in the presence of a lady of respectability, that he had killed more men and ravished more women than any man in America.*
>
> —Washington Irving, American author

TOWARD THE END OF 1778, THE WAR IN THE Northern colonies kind of ground to a halt. General Clinton was hunkered down in New York City waiting for reinforcements from England, and George Washington didn't have enough soldiers to drive Clinton out of there. So Clinton had to look for a new way to approach the war. He sent his best commander, Lord Cornwallis (the British commander at Brandywine and Brooklyn), on a ship with eighty-five hundred soldiers south to the Carolinas. Clinton believed there were a lot of loyalists down there who would be happy to join the war on the side of England. And if Cornwallis could do enough damage, maybe it would force Washington to send some of his men and equipment to deal with it.

So Lord Cornwallis departed New York City, sailed down the coast, and landed his armada at Charleston. He unloaded his troops, barricaded the harbor with warships, laid siege to the city from sea and land, and forced the surrender of all five thousand American soldiers defending the capital of South Carolina. Now he just had to destroy what was left of the rebel army in the South to crush the whole rebellion.

At this point, it's time to talk about the toughest, most ruthless, most hated, and most over-the-top diabolical warrior operating against America during the 1780s: Lieutenant Colonel Banastre Tarleton, better known as "Butcher Tarleton" (and the guy my dad wrote his college thesis on).

"Bloody Ban" was born August 21, 1754, the fourth child of a mayor of Liverpool, England. The mayor was a pretty successful merchant specializing in slaves and sugar, and Banastre studied law at University College in Oxford. Physically smaller than many of the other men in his school, Banastre made up for it by being completely fearless and unwilling to back down from a challenge. He regularly stomped the other kids at cricket, boxing, horseback riding, polo, tennis, and all the other sports you'd expect a privileged British kid to be good at.

Tarleton's dad died shortly after Banastre graduated from Oxford, and since Ban was only the fourth child, all he got from Dad's will was five thousand pounds. This was a pretty sizable chunk of change, but not exactly enough to retire on. Tarleton quickly blew all his money on gambling, booze, parties, and other stuff, then in 1775 spent his last eight hundred pounds to buy an officer's commission in the British Army's First Dragoons Guards. He was immediately shipped out to America to deliver the king's merciful justice to some traitorous colonists who dared defy His Majesty George III.

Back in the old days it was totally cool for a British nobleman to buy himself a rank in the army, but Banastre bought himself the lowest rank in the cavalry (coronet). All his promotions were based on sheer merit (meaning he had to earn them instead of buying higher ranks). He was insanely brave, an excellent horseman and tracker, and absolutely fearless in battle. In December 1776, he was a twenty-three-year-old major, and he was ordered to take a recon party and investigate the operations of Colonial general Charles Lee. At the time, Lee was the second-in-command of the entire Continental Army.

Well, Tarleton didn't just check things out and report back. He attacked. Tarleton personally captured General Lee, who was in his underwear at the time, then hauled him back to base to be interrogated. Later on, Tarleton fought in New York, New Jersey, and Pennsylvania, led a cavalry attack at

the Battle of Brandywine, and was eventually made a lieutenant colonel and given command of his own unit. It was
officially called the "British Legion," but soon came to be
known simply as "Tarleton's Raiders."

Tarleton's Raiders was a group of around five hundred loyalist Americans who weren't down with all that freedom and
independence nonsense. They thought it was far better to be
loyal to the British government than it was to be a bunch of
rebel fighters. Tarleton put British officers in charge, drilled
the loyalists into a proper fighting force, then took them
south with Cornwallis to ruthlessly root out traitors in the
Carolinas.

To give his men extra fighting spirit, Tarleton dressed his cavalrymen in green jackets instead of red coats. Before long, the patriots in Carolina knew that when they saw horsemen in green coats, they were in some serious trouble. Riding on the fastest horses they could find, Tarleton's Raiders were known for daring attacks, even against greater numbers, and for being completely merciless killers who burned the homes and farms of anyone who dared to defy the king of England. They hanged patriot sympathizers, killed prisoners, and recruited loyalists to fight for them.

In one particularly diabolical story, Tarleton went to the home of a guy named Thomas Sumter, who was operating in the wilderness as a commander of the South Carolina Militia. According to the legend, Tarleton introduced himself to Sumter's wife, had dinner with his family and servants, then stood up, politely thanked the family, and ordered his men to torch the entire place. To return the hospitality of Mrs. Sumter, Tarleton placed her favorite chair in the front yard so she could sit in it while she watched her house burn to the ground.

The Raiders were also on the front lines of some serious engagements in the Carolinas. In April 1780, their charge helped break American resistance at the Battle of Monck's Corner, smashing the last of the US cavalry in South Carolina. Only one group survived the battle: the Third Virginia Cavalry, under Abraham Buford (great-uncle of John Buford, hero of the Battle of Gettysburg in the Civil War). Buford had been ordered to fall back and had a ten-day head start on Tarleton, but the British tracker hunted the rebels down, caught up to them, and personally led a charge of around two hundred men head-on into 380 American cavalrymen.

Butcher Tarleton had strict orders to root out all rebels in the Carolinas, and this guy wasn't in the mood to go easy on a force of Americans that outnumbered him two to one. At the Battle of Waxhaws, he attacked Buford's cavalry, decimated them in hand-to-hand combat, then ordered his men to continue firing even after the Americans surrendered. I guess some US dude shot Tarleton's favorite horse out from under him, and he was pretty cheesed off about it. The Americans lost 113 men, with 150 wounded and 53 captured, and the British lost just 19 guys and 31 horses. (Tarleton probably mentions the horses in his memoirs and his after-battle reports because he was still sore about being thrown from his mount while leading a saber charge.)

Of course, with all his brutality, Tarleton wasn't exactly winning over the loyalists in South Carolina. For every horrible thing he did, more men flocked to the patriot cause and joined the militia. Before long, Tarleton's Raiders were so terrifying that Carolinians were joining the army just because they were afraid of what he'd do if he came to their town.

George Washington eventually got tired of this nonsense and sent General Horatio Gates to stop Cornwallis and

Tarleton from demolishing everything in South Carolina. Gates headed south and engaged Cornwallis at the Battle of Camden in August 1780, but once again Tarleton's Raiders proved their skill in combat. At a critical moment in the battle, Tarleton smashed Gates's force with a well-timed sword charge, then personally led the operation to chase fleeing US forces and slash them to death from horseback. He performed similar operations at Fishing Creek and Blackstock Hill later that same month.

With all these epic victories, it made sense that Tarleton would be a little overconfident going into the Battle of Cowpens in January 1781. The dude was twenty-six years old and had spent the last three years bludgeoning the patriots from NYC to Charleston, winning fight after fight no matter how crazy the odds. Unfortunately for Bloody Banastre, this time George Washington sent his toughest commander to deal with the Butcher:

Colonel Daniel Morgan, the big Virginian who had taken on the British at Quebec City and Saratoga.

Morgan had heard of Tarleton's reputation, and he had devised a very specific plan for dealing with him. First, he put his militia units out at the very front of his line. Then Morgan ran through his master plan: The militiamen were to fire two volleys with their rifles, then run away, pretending they were terrified for their lives. Tarleton, being overconfident and glory-hungry, would chase the Americans, hoping to stab them in the back. But he'd run right into a trap, because behind the militia would be a huge group of Continental Army infantrymen waiting with bayonets and loaded muskets to cut his forces apart. Once the regulars fired, the militia would stop fleeing, turn around, and join the fight. Tarleton would be ambushed and surrounded, and his forces would be smashed.

And this is exactly what happened.

It was the first defeat Tarleton ever suffered. Morgan's trap worked perfectly, luring in Tarleton's army and then unleashing fury on him. Tarleton bravely rushed ahead, but when he saw all his men surrendering around him, he and his Raiders ran for it, leaving the broken British Army on the field. Then, just as it almost looked like Tarleton would escape, he was personally attacked by William Washington (remember George's cousin from the Battle of Trenton?) and three hundred of his best cavalry. Tarleton was nearly captured, but even though he was badly outnumbered he cut his way through the enemy in an intense sword fight on horseback. Tarleton even personally wounded Washington in the fight. To keep up his spoiled-rich-kid cred, Tarleton would forever say that his defeat at Cowpens was Cornwallis's fault (which I love) because Cornwallis didn't provide him with adequate reinforcements.

When Lord Cornwallis heard about the defeat at Cowpens, he was furious. He rode out with Tarleton to fight the Continental Army once more and ran into an American force

under Nathanael Greene at Guilford Courthouse in North Carolina in March 1781. Cornwallis and Tarleton drove the Americans from the field in a battle that took an entire day, but their victory came at a terrible cost: Greene's forces killed or wounded nearly a quarter of Cornwallis's army, and two of Tarleton's fingers were shot off while he was dueling with American cavalry. He lived to tell the tale, of course.

At that same battle, our six-foot-six-inch giant friend Peter Francisco ("the Virginia Hercules") is credited with killing a few more British soldiers with his broadsword before finally passing out. He had been stabbed multiple times with bayonets and swords. But Francisco lived, crawling his way to a nearby farmhouse to recover from a dozen or so incredibly serious wounds. Tarleton's Raiders traveled there to finish the job on the Virginia Hercules, but Francisco killed one of Tarleton's captains with the guy's own cavalry saber, chopped another loyalist soldier's hand off, and stole their horses.

Despite all the brutality and all the victories Cornwallis and Tarleton had won in the Carolinas, in the end they had completely failed to break the fighting spirit of the Carolinians. Every horrible act the Raiders pulled just made the Americans want to fight harder. Before long, the British and loyalists found themselves in a situation where they simply didn't have enough men left to continue fighting, while the patriots kept getting more and more fresh recruits to their cause. After Guilford Courthouse, Cornwallis finally ordered his troops to fall back to Wilmington, North Carolina, board ships, and head north toward Virginia.

But the Americans weren't about to let him get away that easily.

Frontier Justice

Three months before the Battle of Cowpens, another vicious Brit got what was coming to him as well, this time in one of the weirdest battles in military history. Major Patrick Ferguson, a man who truly despised the rebels, went out and recruited a force of around a thousand loyalist American Tories. Swearing to "lay waste to their country with fire and sword," Ferguson's men stormed around South Carolina burning homes, plundering plantations, killing civilians, destroying crops, and killing livestock.

Well, this didn't sit too well with the locals, and out of nowhere, a group of nine hundred "Overmountain Men" (including Davy Crockett's dad!) arrived from Kentucky, Tennessee, and the Carolinas. They tracked Ferguson to his base on King's Mountain, where he was caught completely off guard by their super-accurate sniper fire. But every time he ran out with bayonets, the Overmountain Men just hid behind rocks and trees and kept right on shooting. Ferguson was shot eight times, and when he died, the surviving men in his command surrendered. The Overmountain Men recognized a few of their loyalist prisoners, hanged nine men for the crime of murdering civilians, and then went home, never to be heard from again.

THE VILLAIN ESCAPED?

Unlike the fate of many villains in big-time action movies, this real-life story doesn't end with the bad guy dying. Far from it. After the Revolution, Tarleton went home to England and was knighted, promoted, and elected to Parliament, where he became a vocal advocate for not ending the slave trade (seriously, the guy was evil). Known as Sir Banastre Tarleton, First Baronet, "Bloody Ban" wrote his best-selling memoirs and then spent fifteen years dating the most famous actress in England. (He only went out with her because a friend bet him that he couldn't get a girl that pretty.) He lived to be seventy-eight and died a wealthy and successful man. Blech.

Know Your Founding Fathers

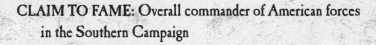

NAME: Nathanael Greene

BIRTHDAY: August 7, 1742

BIRTHPLACE: Warwick, Rhode Island

CLAIM TO FAME: Overall commander of American forces in the Southern Campaign

JOB BEFORE THE WAR: Owned a foundry

ROLE IN THE WAR: One of Washington's most trusted subordinate officers, he commanded troops from Boston to Carolina.

AFTER THE WAR: Greene retired to a large estate in Georgia, just north of Savannah. He was offered the position of secretary of war twice, but refused both times.

BONUS FACT: Greene walked with a very pronounced limp. He was a Quaker, a religion that preaches nonviolence, and because of his involvement with the war the Quakers kicked him out of their religion.

Yorktown

The Battle of Chesapeake Capes

Chesapeake Capes, Virginia
September 5, 1781

> We must take Cornwallis or be all dishonored.
>
> —George Washington

TARLETON AND CORNWALLIS'S MAJOR defeats at King's Mountain, Cowpens, and Guilford Courthouse had cost them nearly all their troops, so now they needed to get out of Carolina and regroup. Cornwallis marched his large army to the coast, reloaded his ships at Wilmington, North Carolina, and set sail for the Chesapeake Bay and Virginia. There he linked up with another familiar face, British Army brigadier general Benedict Arnold, and the three redcoat officers headed out into Virginia to wreak havoc. In the spring of 1781, Arnold captured Richmond and burned a huge stockpile of American supplies. Tarleton rode with his Raiders out to Charlottesville, almost captured Thomas Jefferson, and plundered Jefferson's house.

Daniel Morgan and Nathanael Greene were still tying up loose ends in the Carolinas, so George Washington sent three of his toughest dudes out to deal with the threat in Virginia. In 1781, the Marquis de Lafayette, "Mad" Anthony Wayne, and Baron Friedrich von Steuben all marched south to face the enemy in an epic Texas Tornado battle.

Lafayette was in charge of the American operation, and knowing that he was massively outnumbered by the British, he came up with a simple but effective plan: Just don't get involved in a huge fight with the redcoats. Try to contain them. Push them back. Buy time.

Lafayette, von Steuben, and Wayne fought a few battles here and there, wearing Cornwallis, Arnold, and Tarleton down. Before long, the British were running out of supplies, food, and manpower. The ninety-five hundred surviving redcoats fell back to the fortress coastal city of Yorktown, Virginia. There they dug a huge network of trenches, set up defensive cannon positions, and waited for a gigantic shipment of soldiers, weapons, guns, food, and ammo to arrive on a humongous naval convoy from England. Then Cornwallis could decide whether to strike at Lafayette with an overwhelmingly powerful army or simply board his ships and sail north to New York City so he could link back up with Clinton and the rest of the British Army.

There was one thing, however, that Lord Cornwallis didn't expect.

On August 30, 1781, he woke up in his headquarters, looked out the window to the Chesapeake Bay, and saw a fleet of twenty-four French warships sailing into the harbor.

Washington's spies had been effective yet again, and the American commander knew exactly what the British were planning to do. He couldn't let Cornwallis escape with half the British Army, so Washington had requested a French blockade of Yorktown, left a small army in New Jersey to face Clinton, and then took twenty-five hundred Continentals and four thousand French soldiers south to surround Cornwallis. Together with the French commander,

Jean-Baptiste-Donatien de Vimeur, Count de Rochambeau, the Continental Army marched two hundred miles in fifteen days, linked up with Lafayette's force, and marched straight for Yorktown with a force nearly twice the size of the British.

Cornwallis was about to be trapped.

There was only one way out of this: straight through that dang French fleet sitting in Chesapeake Bay. Cornwallis put out a desperate call for help, and on September 5, 1781, ten days after the French arrived, a large British fleet under Rear Admiral Thomas Graves appeared on the horizon. It consisted of nineteen Royal Navy vessels, mounting fourteen hundred cannons, all helmed and crewed by the greatest sailors, gunners, and marines the world had ever seen.

The French fleet, twenty-four ships and 1,788 cannons commanded by Admiral François-Joseph-Paul, Comte de Grasse, turned hard toward the horizon, ran up the battle sails, and got ready to engage.

It's worth mentioning here that the most important and most decisive battle of the American Revolution did not involve a single American soldier, sailor, or marine. If you can believe it, this was all French and Brits.

Admiral de Grasse ordered his ships into a battle line. He had more ships and more guns, but his crews were not nearly as experienced as the British. He knew he would have to play it carefully. So he ordered his men to maneuver toward the wind, and his two- and three-decked wooden sailing ships slammed open their gunports. French gun crews barked out commands as heavy iron cannon carriages wheeled forward, running out row after row of black muzzles. The British responded, forcing their way into a line, their crews expertly climbing the rigging, pulling ropes, tacking sails, and lining up in perfect formation. The British ran out their guns in unison.

Within minutes, the ships pulled up in a perfect line across from each other. If you were watching it from space, it would look like an equal sign (=), with each line firing at the other with seven hundred to eight hundred cannons all at the same time.

Explosions rippled up and down the lines as cannonballs smashed home. Sails were punctured, damaging speed and maneuverability. Officers screamed on quarterdecks, giving orders as explosions blasted all around them. Ships caught fire or splintered into wooden shrapnel that laced across the decks and cut men down. In the gun decks, cramped in the heat, gun crews on both sides worked frantically to load their weapons and fire, even as enemy shells struck home and exploded farther down the deck. Above, French and British marines loaded muskets, firing volleys into enemy ships or swinging swivel guns to spray shotgun blasts of grapeshot. The ships came so close you could see the men on the other boat without a telescope.

The engagement lasted two hours. As darkness fell, ending

the fight, 336 British and 221 French sailors lay dead or wounded on their decks. The British ship *Terrible* was sinking, unable to be repaired, and rescue boats were desperately trying to pull men out of the smashed wreckage. Admiral Samuel Hood grimly surveyed his situation and made the difficult decision to save his fleet at the cost of Cornwallis's army.

When dawn broke back at Yorktown, a massive cheer arose all across the American and French lines as a badly damaged fleet of twenty-four French warships sailed back into Chesapeake Bay.

The main body of George Washington's force arrived soon after on October 6, 1781. General Henry Knox organized the fifty-six French and American cannons, ordering barrage after barrage to smash into the Yorktown defenses. Cornwallis attempted a counterattack, but his most trusted commander, Banastre Tarleton, was wounded in a sword fight with French cavalry and was forced to fall back to Yorktown. Over the next few days, daring nighttime bayonet attacks led by American colonel Alexander Hamilton and a large battalion of French infantry overran the outer defenses at Yorktown, capturing a few key trenches.

It was over, and the British knew it.

General Lord Cornwallis officially requested a cease-fire from George Washington on October 17, 1781. Two days later he agreed to the unconditional surrender of all the British soldiers under his command. In an instant, half of the British Army in North America became prisoners of war.

The war officially went on until 1783, but the surrender of Cornwallis's force at Yorktown was the last major battle of the American Revolution. Without those troops, Henry Clinton could not continue his fight, and with engagements now going on all over the world, King George realized he was finished.

The United States of America, once just a pipe dream of some upset Boston colonists, was now about to become a reality. For all the hardships, the defeats, the long winters, and

Postage stamp commemorating the Battle of Yorktown

the horrible brutality, the patriots had persevered through the most intense of struggles and had emerged victorious.

America was now a free country, independent of the British Empire and at liberty to govern itself.

I DIDN'T WANT TO GO TO YOUR STUPID PARTY ANYWAY

It was customary in the good old days of military gentlemanship for victorious generals to invite their defeated counterparts to dinner after the war, and this is exactly what happened after the surrender at Yorktown. Cornwallis and his staff sat down and ate a super-fancy dinner provided by the French and American generals, and everyone had nice polite conversation and tried not to talk too much about how they'd all been trying to kill each other recently. But as an awesome postwar side note, the only British officer who did not receive a formal invitation to dinner after Yorktown was Brigadier General Banastre Tarleton (Benedict Arnold fled for England before the British surrender at Yorktown, but I can't imagine anyone in America was too excited about the idea of offering him a steak dinner, either).

THE SPANISH PIRATE ARMADA

One truly unsung hero of the American Revolution was Admiral Bernardo de Gálvez, the Spanish governor of Louisiana. When the Revolution began, Gálvez attacked British shipping along the Mississippi River, running supplies and gear to the Americans even though the Spanish hadn't officially declared war on England yet. Once Spain declared war on England, Gálvez put out a call for able-bodied soldiers to join him. He built an army of Spanish troops, French settlers, free blacks, runaway slaves, Texans, Mexicans, pirates, and anyone else he could find, then set out to fight the British. Commanding a fleet of ships and nearly two thousand soldiers, Gálvez set sail from New Orleans and captured British forts at Mobile, Alabama; Pensacola and Key West, Florida; and the Bahamas; and he was preparing an assault on Jamaica when the war ended. Nowadays, the city of Galveston, Texas, is named after him.

AWW, YOU SHOULDN'T HAVE

To celebrate the one hundredth anniversary of American independence, the French government financed the construction of a gigantic statue commemorating the French-American alliance that led to victory. It was designed by French sculptor

Frédéric-Auguste Bartholdi, built by Gustave Eiffel (the guy who built the Eiffel Tower), and presented as a gift by the people of France. Standing 151 feet tall and made of solid copper, the statue depicts Libertas, the Roman goddess of liberty, holding a torch in one hand. In the other, she holds a tablet inscribed JULY 4, 1776. When the statue arrived on a ship from France in 1886, it was paraded (still in pieces) through the streets in New York City's first ticker-tape parade. It was then assembled, mounted on a pedestal, and displayed outside New York Harbor, where it greets travelers to this day. The French titled the statue *La Liberté éclairant le monde* (meaning Liberty Enlightening the World), but we know it better as the Statue of Liberty. Here's a fun fact, though: She wasn't always green! When Lady Liberty was originally displayed, she was the same color as a brand-new penny. The green comes from years of oxidization of the copper she's made of (ask your science teacher how this works).

Know Your Founding Fathers

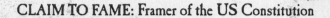

NAME: Alexander Hamilton

BIRTHDAY: January 11, 1755

BIRTHPLACE: Charlestown, Nevis

CLAIM TO FAME: Framer of the US Constitution

JOB BEFORE THE WAR: Clerk, writer

ROLE IN THE WAR: Aide to George Washington, commanded troops at the Battles of Trenton and Yorktown

AFTER THE WAR: Was one of the most influential framers of the US Constitution; secretary of the Treasury from 1789 to 1795

BONUS FACT: Hamilton was killed in a duel by Aaron Burr, who was the vice president of the United States at the time of the gunfight. Hamilton had ticked Burr off by writing some mean newspaper articles about him, but Hamilton didn't expect a for-real fight. Hamilton fired his pistol up in the air, "throwing away his shot" as was the custom for a gentlemanly, nonkilling duel. Burr shot Hamilton in the gut, killing him.

Conclusion

Building a Nation

> We the People of the United States, in Order to form a more perfect Union, establish Justice, insure domestic Tranquility, provide for the common defence, promote the general Welfare, and secure the Blessings of Liberty to ourselves and our Posterity, do ordain and establish this Constitution for the United States of America.
>
> —Preamble to the United States Constitution

W HEN THE BRITISH PRIME MINISTER, Lord North, heard the news of Yorktown, he reacted "as he would have taken a ball in his breast." He knew it was over. He resigned, effective immediately, and in 1782, the British Parliament voted to end the war and grant America its independence. The last British troops boarded ships and departed New York City on November 25, 1783.

America sent Ben Franklin, John Adams, and future Supreme Court justice John Jay to Paris to negotiate the terms of the treaty with Great Britain. America gained independence for the thirteen colonies and received the Northwest Territories (thanks to George Rogers Clark), Spain got Florida, and Britain got to keep the Bahamas, even though Spain had captured it. America agreed to stop patriots from stealing property from loyalists. Canada stayed with England. Both the United States and Great Britain were allowed to use the Mississippi River (the British were using it to get supplies to and from the interior of Canada) and go fishing off the coast of Newfoundland. There were a few other terms, I guess, but none of it was too exciting. One funny thing that happened was that the Continental Congress made John Adams leave Paris soon after he arrived. Adams hated the French so much that the Congress were worried he was jeopardizing the mission. Adams ended up writing a bunch of awesome letters about how we should go to war with France next. I find this hilarious.

Now that the war was won, it was time to actually, you know, figure out what the heck this new country was going to look like. The Second Continental Congress had set up a document called the Articles of Confederation back in 1777, because the Americans had been scared of trading one overbearing horrible tyrant for another. So the Articles basically

Signing the Preliminary Treaty of Peace at Paris, November 30, 1782, printed by John D. Morris & Co. after a painting by Carl Wilhelm Anton Seiler

gave all the power to the thirteen states and set up Congress to kind of oversee everything (but not do too much).

By 1785, however, it was pretty clear this wasn't going to work. The federal government (Congress) was just too weak under that setup. Each state could derail any kind of federal bill, and it was impossible to get the states to agree on anything. So nothing got done and it was total chaos everywhere. The government was broke, farmers were rebelling, the currency was worthless, and it got so crazy that France and

Spain were negotiating treaties with individual states instead of with America as a whole.

America needed something else, so in 1787, a group led by Alexander Hamilton and James Madison met to figure out a better system of government. Fifty-five delegates from twelve states (Rhode Island told the group to jump in a lake) met at Independence Hall in Philadelphia to set up a United States Constitution that put in place the system of laws for the new country. Basically, they set up three branches of government: a chief executive (the president), a legislature (two groups—a Senate that gave each state the same number of votes, and a House of Representatives that gave each state a number of votes based on the number of people who lived there), and a Supreme Court (to make legal decisions).

In theory, each of these groups had an equal amount of power, and any one could block the others from doing something stupid or un-American that would compromise the freedom of the country. Sure, it might not have been perfect, but you also have to consider that nobody had ever tried anything like this before! The fact that this Constitution is still around over two hundred years later should tell you that they did a pretty dang good job with it.

The United States Constitution was signed on September 17, 1787. A Bill of Rights (the first ten amendments) was added shortly after. George Washington was elected the first president of the United States of America, with John Adams as his vice president, and Washington took office on April 30, 1789. He remains the only president in history to be unanimously elected by the Electoral College.

Of course, in the grand scheme of things, the American Revolution didn't just set up the United States of America and begin a new system of government. Its results were even more far-reaching than that. You see, helping us out in the war kind of taxed the French government, and before long the people of France (who had written most of the Enlightenment literature that inspired America to begin with) were like, "Hey, why do we still have a king?" In 1789—the same year the United States Constitution went into effect—the people of France launched a revolution of their own. Guided by their document of freedom, the Declaration of the Rights of Man and of the Citizen, the French overthrew their king and went about trying to set up a democratic republic.

Well...this ended up being a heck of a struggle for the French as well. Sure, they were overthrowing their king and not fighting to break away from an existing empire, but the French Republic scared the crap out of the other kingdoms of Europe. Before long, France was at war with England, Prussia, Austria, Russia, Spain, Portugal, the Ottoman Empire, Holland, Ireland, and most of the Italian states pretty much all at the same time. Luckily for the French, they had a previously unknown military commander named Napoleon Bonaparte fighting on their side (although that is *definitely* a tale for a different book). They also had internal problems, which turned into the Reign of Terror, when King Louis XVI and Queen Marie Antoinette (plus *tons* of other people, mostly nobles) had their heads chopped off by a guillotine, and this wasn't a whole lot of fun for anyone.

As a related side note, our friend the Marquis de Lafayette played a pretty major role in the French Revolution. He was a coauthor of the Declaration of the Rights of Man and of the Citizen, commanded the Parisian National Guard, saved Marie Antoinette's life once, and ultimately ended up being arrested during the Reign of Terror because he wasn't superdown with lopping off *all* the aristocrats' heads and kind of wanted to find something in between "monarchy forever" and "kill all nobility." Napoleon eventually busted him out of prison, and Lafayette spent the rest of his life living in a huge, awesome mansion, where he helped French and Polish refugees escape execution at the hands of murderous revolutionaries.

The ideas of liberty and equality resonated in other places on the American side of the Atlantic as well. Just twenty years after the Constitution, there were colonial rebellions against the French in Haiti and against the Spanish in Mexico and in South America. Among the notable heroes of these revolutions was Símon Bolívar, who is credited with personally liberating the countries of Venezuela, Colombia, Panama, Ecuador, Peru, and Bolivia from the Kingdom of Spain. Bolívar was a huge admirer of George Washington and Thomas Jefferson and wanted to model his liberated countries on the ideals of the American Revolution.

In the end, the American Revolution was a long, bloody war that cost the lives of many valiant men and women on both sides of the conflict. It was an epic struggle for freedom and independence, full of daring battles and heroic deeds, but it was also the beginning of a new era of human history, one in which the ancient ways of medieval kings were replaced by new, forward-thinking ideas about individual freedom, equality, reason, free speech, and national independence. It brought forth into the world a new country, one that would take a prominent role in world politics in the centuries to come, and marked the beginning of a world where the citizens of a country are free to govern themselves in a truly democratic society.

And that is a legacy I know all Americans can be proud of.

Acknowledgments

My brave fellows, you have done all I asked you to do, and more than can be reasonably expected; but your country is at stake, your wives, your houses and all that you hold dear. You have worn yourselves out with fatigues and hardships, but we know not how to spare you. If you will consent to stay one month longer, you will render that service to the cause of liberty, and to your country, which you probably can never do under any other circumstances.

—George Washington

THIS BOOK IS DEDICATED TO ALL MY FAMILY and friends, for your unending support through everything that life has to offer. There have been some very difficult times for me, and you have always been there. I appreciate it more than I can say.

Thank you to my mom and my dad, for all your support, and to my brothers, John and Clay, and my sisters, Barbara and Scarlet. To my uncle Fred, for digging up our family's

Revolutionary War history, and to Brian Snoddy for helping me try to solve all the world's problems.

Thank you to my amazing editor, Deirdre Jones, for all her wonderful help promoting, editing, and championing the book, to her assistant, Kheryn Callender, and to my agents, Farley Chase of Chase Literary and Sean Daily of Hotchkiss, for continually believing in me. To my copy editor, Barbara Perris, for correcting all my terrible grammar, and also to my fact checker, Jody Revenson, a self-proclaimed "insufferable know-it-all" who fact-checked me before I fact-wrecked myself, yet dared to mention that there's still some debate over whether or not Han Shot First (spoiler: He did). My sincerest gratitude also goes out to Alyssa Isaacks, the self-proclaimed (but 100 percent accurately titled) "Best Intern Ever."

And thank you to all of you out there reading this, commenting on the Guts & Glory Facebook page, or sending me kind letters. Without your fantastic support, none of this could ever happen.

Bibliography

As our enemies have found we can reason like men, so now let us show them we can fight like men also.

—Thomas Jefferson

GENERAL BOOKS USED THROUGHOUT

Axelrod, Alan. *The Real History of the American Revolution*. New York: Stirling, 2007.

Chambers, John Whiteclay II. *The Oxford Companion to American Military History*. New York: Oxford University Press, 1999.

Duvall, Kathleen. *Independence Lost: Lives on the Edge of the American Revolution*. New York: Random House, 2015.

Lancaster, Bruce. *The American Revolution*. New York: American Heritage, 1971.

Lanning, Michael Lee. *The American Revolution 100*. Naperville, IL: Sourcebooks, 2009.

Nester, William. *The Revolutionary Years, 1775–1789*. Washington, DC: Potomac, 2011.

Sandler, Stanley. *Ground Warfare: An International Encyclopedia*. Santa Barbara, CA: ABC-CLIO, 2002.

COOL WEBSITES YOU CAN VISIT

www.britishbattles.com

www.history.com/topics/american-revolution

www.revolutionarywaranimated.com

www.ushistory.org/us/index.asp

www.mountvernon.org/digital-encyclopedia/subject/american-revolution

www.nps.gov/revwar

ADDITIONAL SOURCES

The Sons of Liberty

Alexander, John K. *Samuel Adams: Life of an American Revolutionary.* Lanham, MD: Rowman & Littlefield, 2011.

Irvin, Benjamin. *Samuel Adams: Son of Liberty, Father of Revolution.* New York: Oxford University Press, 2002.

Robertson, Andrew W. *Encyclopedia of U.S. Political History.* Washington, DC: CQ Press, 2010.

Simmons, George A. "Samuel Adams." *The Pennsylvania Magazine of History and Biography*, Vol. 1, pp. 431–443. Philadelphia: The Historical Society of Pennsylvania, 1877.

The Shot Heard Round the World

Fremont-Barnes, Gregory. *Encyclopedia of the Age of Political Revolutions and New Ideologies, 1760–1815.* Westport, CT: Greenwood Press, 2007.

Samuels, Charles. *The Battles of Lexington and Concord.* New York: Gareth Stevens Publishing, 2014.

Bunker Hill

Fortescue, Sir John. *A History of the British Army.* East Sussex, UK: The Naval & Military Press, Ltd., 2004.

Horwitz, Tony. "The True Story of the Battle of Bunker Hill." *Smithsonian Magazine*, May 2013.

Risjord, Norman K. *Jefferson's America, 1760–1815*. Lanham, MD: Rowman & Littlefield, 2010.

Ward, Christopher. *The War of the Revolution*. New York: Macmillan, 1952.

Building the Continental Army

Billias, George Athan. *George Washington's Generals and Opponents*. Cambridge, MA: Da Capo Press, 1994.

Brooks, Noah. *Henry Knox, a Soldier of the Revolution*. New York: G. P. Putnam, 1900.

Puls, Mark. *Henry Knox*. New York: Palgrave Macmillan, 2008.

The Invasion of Canada

Desjardin, Thomas A. *Through a Howling Wilderness*. New York: St. Martin's Griffin, 2007.

Lefkowitz, Arthur S. *Benedict Arnold's Army*. New York: Savas Beattie, 2008.

Mays, Terry M. *Historical Dictionary of the American Revolution*. Lanham, MD: Scarecrow Press, 2010.

Morrissey, Brendan. *Quebec 1775*. Oxford: Osprey Publishing Ltd., 2003.

Wood, W. J. *Battles of the Revolutionary War, 1775–1781*. Chapel Hill, NC: Algonquin Books of Chapel Hill, 1990.

The Empire Strikes Back

Gallagher, John J. *The Battle of Brooklyn, 1776*. Cambridge, MA: Da Capo Press, 1995.

Van Buskirk, Judith L. *Generous Enemies: Patriots and Loyalists in Revolutionary New York*. Philadelphia: University of Philadelphia Press, 2004.

Crossing the Delaware

Davis, Paul K. *100 Decisive Battles: From Ancient Times to the Present*. New York: Oxford University Press, 2001.

Fischer, David Hackett. *Washington's Crossing*. New York: Oxford University Press, 2004.

Ketchum, Richard M. *The Winter Soldiers: The Battles for Trenton and Princeton*. New York: Henry Holt and Company, 2014.

McCullough, David. *Seventeen Seventy-six*. New York: Simon & Schuster, 2006.

Sutherland, Jonathan. *African-Americans at War: Vol. 1*. Santa Barbara, CA: ABC-CLIO, 2004.

The Marquis de Lafayette

"Casimir Pulaski." *American Monthly Magazine*, Vol. 37, August 1910.

Denslow, William R., and Harry S. Truman. *10,000 Famous Freemasons from A to Z*. Whitefish, MT: Kessinger Publishing, 1959.

Griffin, Martin Ignatius Joseph. *Catholics and the American Revolution*. Ridley Park, PA: Published by the author, 1911.

Saratoga

Ketchum, Richard M. *Saratoga: Turning Point of America's Revolutionary War*. New York: Henry Holt & Company, 2014.

Lanning, Michael Lee. *The Battle 100: The stories behind history's most influential battles*. Naperville, IL: Sourcebooks, 2005.

MacDonald, John. *Great Battlefields of the World*. New York: Collier Books, 1984.

Morrissey, Brendan. *Saratoga 1777: Turning Point of a Revolution*. Oxford: Osprey Publishing Ltd., 2000.

Sneiderman, Barney. *Warriors Seven*. New York: Savas Beattie, 2006.

Valley Forge

Adelson, Bruce. *Baron von Steuben: American General*. New York: Chelsea House, 2013.

Lockhart, Paul Douglas. *The Drillmaster of Valley Forge*. New York: Collins, 2008.

Lyons, Reneé Critcher. *Foreign-born American Patriots*. Jefferson, NC: McFarland & Company, Inc., 2014.

The Legend of Molly Pitcher

Burke, Rick. *Molly Pitcher*. Chicago: Heinemann Library, 2003.

De Pauw, Linda Grant. *In Search of Molly Pitcher*. Pasadena, MD: Peacock Press, 2007.

Glaser, Jason, et al. *Molly Pitcher: Young American Patriot*. Mankato, MN: Capstone Press, 2006.

Pierce, Grace M. "Three American Women Pensioned for Military Service." *Daughters of the American Revolution Magazine*, Vol. 50–51, January 1917.

"Mad" Anthony and the Virginia Hercules

Trudeau, Noah Andre. "Battle of Stony Point." *MHQ: The Quarterly Journal of Military History*, Fall 2003.

The Culper Ring

Allen, Thomas B., and Cheryl Harness. *George Washington, Spymaster*. Washington, DC: National Geographic Society, 2004.

Carlisle, Rodney. *Encyclopedia of Intelligence and Counterintelligence*. Vol. 1–2. New York: Taylor & Francis, 2005.

Frank, Lisa Tendrich. *An Encyclopedia of American Women at War*. Santa Barbara, CA: ABC-CLIO, 2013.

Kilmeade, Brian, and Don Yaeger. *George Washington's Secret Six*. New York: Sentinel, 2014.

Misencik, Paul R. *The Original American Spies*. Jefferson, NC: McFarland & Company, 2014.

Not Yet Begun to Fight

Collum, Richard S. *History of the United States Marine Corps*. New York: L. R. Hammersley, 1903.

Selby, John. *United States Marine Corps*. London: Osprey Publishing Ltd., 2014.

Deborah Sampson

Kneib, Martha. *Women Soldiers, Spies, and Patriots of the American Revolution*. New York: Rosen Publishing Group, 2003.

Wells, Kate Gannet. "Deborah Sampson, A Heroine of the American Revolution." *The Bay State Monthly*, Vol. 13, February 1896.

Young, Alfred. *Masquerade: The Life and Times of Deborah Sampson, Continental Soldier*. New York: Vintage Books, 2005.

Image Credits

Page 7: Courtesy of the *National Atlas of the United States.* Page 23: Courtesy of the Library of Congress. Page 37: Henry Hudson Kitson, Courtesy of Daderot. Page 56: E. Percy Moran, Courtesy of the Library of Congress. Page 74: Courtesy of the National Archives. Page 78: Lexicon, Vikrum. Page 79, top and bottom: Hoshie. Page 80, top: DevinCook, jacobolus. Page 80, bottom: Zippanova. Page 85: Henry Bryan Hall, Sr., after a painting by John Trumbull, Courtesy of the National Archives. Page 121: Dmadeo. Page 132: Courtesy of the United States Military Academy. Page 144: Joseph-Désiré Court, Courtesy of the Réunion des Musées Nationaux. Page 161: Charles Willson Peale, Courtesy of the National Park Service Museum Collections. Page 176: Charles Willson Peale, Courtesy of the Pennsylvania Academy of the Fine Arts. Page 186: David Martin, Courtesy of the White House Historical Association. Page 197: Courtesy of the United States Military Academy. Page 208: Trumbull and Forest, Courtesy of the Library of Congress. Page 233: Americasroof. Page 244: Gwillhickers, Courtesy of the United States Post

Office and the Bureau of Engraving and Printing. Page 268: George Graham, William Beastall, Joseph Stone, Courtesy of the Massachusetts Historical Society. Page 291: Gwillhickers, Courtesy of the United States Post Office and the Bureau of Engraving and Printing. Page 298: John D. Morris & Co., Carl Wilhelm Anton Seiler, Courtesy of the U.S. Diplomacy Center.

Index

Page numbers in italics refer to images, photographs, and illustrations in the text.